SCREENING EUROPE

Image and '*ntity in Contemporary European Cinema*

Edited by

BFI PUBLISHING

First published in 1992 by the
British Film Institute
21 Stephen Street
London W1P 1PL

Copyright © British Film Institute 1992

British Library Cataloguing in Publication Data
Screening Europe: Image and Identity in Contemporary European
Cinema – (BFI Working Papers)
 I. Petrie, Duncan J. II. Series
 791.43094

 ISBN 0–85170–321–6

Cover design by Roger Walton

Typeset in 10 on 11.5pt Sabon by
Fakenham Photosetting Limited,
Fakenham, Norfolk
and printed in Great Britain by
St Edmundsbury Press,
Bury St Edmunds, Suffolk

CONTENTS

NOTES ON CONTRIBUTORS

Chantal Akerman Innovative and prolific Belgian film-maker, influenced by Godard and American experimental film-makers Stan Brakhage, Michael Snow and Jonas Mekas. Films include *Hotel Monterey* 1973, *Je, tu, il, elle* 1974, *Jeanne Dielman, 23 Quai du Commerce, 1080 Bruxelles* 1975, *News from Home* 1976, *Les Rendez-vous d'Anna* 1978, *Toute une nuit* 1982, *Les Anées 80* 1983, *Jour Pina a demandé* 1983, *Family Business* 1984, *Histoires d'Amérique* 1989, *Nuit et Jour* 1990.

John Akomfrah Born in Ghana but has lived most of his life in London. Founder member of the Black Audio Film Collective in 1983, he has worked on multimedia projects and films for the collective including *Handsworth Songs* 1986, *Sanctuary Challenge* 1987, *Testament* 1988 and *Who Needs a Heart?* 1991.

Ien Ang Lecturer in the School of Humanities, Murdock University, Australia. Ien has published several articles and books on the media, including *Watching Dallas: Soap Opera and the Melodramatic Imagination* and *Desperately Seeking the Audience*.

John Caughie Senior Lecturer in Film and Television Studies at the University of Glasgow, and co-director of the John Logie Baird Centre. His publications include *Theories of Authorship* and *Television: Ideology and Exchange*, together with a number of articles on television theory and history and on Scottish film culture. He is an editor of *Screen*.

Antoine Compagnon Professor of French at Columbia University, New York.

Nancy Condee and **Vladimir Padunov** Members of the Slavic Department, University of Pittsburgh, they write on Soviet cultural politics. Their work has appeared in *The Nation*, the *New York Times*, the *Harriman Forum*, *October*, *Framework*, and the Soviet journal *Questions of Literature*.

iv

Claire Denis Brought up in a French colonial family in West Africa, she has worked with Wim Wenders, Jim Jarmusch, Costa Gavras and Dusan Makavejev before directing her first film, *Chocolat* 1988. Other films include *Man No Run* (Documentary) 1989 and *S'en fout la mort* 1990.

Philip Dodd Editor of the recently relaunched *Sight and Sound*. Was formerly deputy editor of *New Statesman and Society* and an academic for fifteen years. He co-edited *Englishness: Politics and Culture 1880–1920*, co-authored *Relative Values: or what's art worth?* and has written widely on art, film and nationalism. For five years he has been consultant to Music and Arts, BBC Television. He is currently writing a two-hundred-year history of Englishness, *True Stories 1789–1989*.

Jean-Luc Godard Seminal French film-maker, leading light of the *nouvelle vague*. His canon includes *A bout de souffle* 1959, *Le Petit Soldat* 1960, *Une Femme est une femme* 1961, *Vivre sa vie* 1962, *Les Carabiniers* 1963, *Le Mépris* 1963, *Bande à part* 1964, *Une Femme mariée* 1964, *Alphaville* 1965, *Pierrot le fou* 1965, *Made in the USA* 1966, *Deux ou trois choses que je sais d'elle* 1966, *La Chinoise* 1967, *Weekend* 1967, *Le Gai Savoir* 1968, *Un Film comme les autres* 1968, *One Plus One* 1968, *British Sounds* 1969, *Pravda* 1969, *Vent d'est* 1969, *Luttes en Italie* 1969, *Vladimir et Rosa* 1971, *Tout va bien* 1972, *Letter to Jane* 1972, *Ici et ailleurs* 1974, *Numéro deux* 1975, *Comment ça va?* 1975, *Sauve qui peut la vie* 1979, *Passion* 1981, *Prenom: Carmen* 1982, *Je vous salue Marie* 1983, *Detective* 1984, *Grandeur et décadence du petit commerce du cinéma* 1986, *King Lear* 1987, *Soigne ta droite* 1987, *Visages suisse* 1989, *Nouvelle vague* 1990.

Stuart Hall Professor of Sociology at the Open University, he was formerly director of the pioneering Centre for Contemporary Cultural Studies in Birmingham from 1974 to 1979. His books include *The Popular Arts* (co-editor), *Culture, Media, Language* (co-editor) and *The Hard Road to Renewal: Thatcherism and the Crisis on the Left*.

Fredric Jameson Professor of Comparative Literature and Professor of French, Duke University, Durham, North Carolina. His numerous publications include: *Sartre: The Origins of a Style*, *Marxism and Form: Twentieth Century Dialectical Theories of Literature*, *The Prison-house of Language*, *Fables of Aggression: Wyndham Lewis, The Modernist as Fascist*, *The Political Unconscious*, *Postmodernism* *and Cultural Theories* (Lectures in China), *The Ideology of Theory, Essays 1971–1986, Messages of the Visible: Film/Theory/ Periodization, The Concept of Postmodernism, Dialectical Aesthetics* and *Postmodernism, or the Cultural Logic of Late Capitalism.*

Isaac Julien A graduate of St Martins School of Art, he was a founding member of Sankofa film and video in the early eighties. His films include *Who Killed Colin Roach?* 1983, *Passion of Remembrance* 1986, *Looking for Langston* 1989, and *Young Soul Rebels* 1990.

Patrizia Lombardo Professor of French and Italian at the University of Pittsburgh, she has taught in Italy, France and America. Her publications include *Edgar Allan Poe et la modernité: Breton, Barthes, Derrida, Blanchot, The Three Paradoxes of Roland Barthes* and the forthcoming *H. Taine and the Battle of Disciplines.*

Colin MacCabe Head of Research BFI and Professor of English, University of Pittsburgh. Numerous books and articles include *Godard: Images, Sounds, Politics* and *High Theory/Low Culture.* Previously Head of BFI Production, where he was Executive Producer on *Caravaggio* (Derek Jarman 1986), *Friendship's Death* (Peter Wollen 1987), *On the Black Hill* (Andrew Grieve 1988), *Distant Voices, Still Lives* (Terence Davis 1988), *Venus Peter* (Ian Sellar 1989), *Play Me Something* (Timothy Neat and John Berger 1989), *Hallelujah Anyhow* (Matthew Jacobs 1990) and *Young Soul Rebels* (Isaac Julien 1991). He was producer on *Melancholia* (Andi Engel 1989) and Executive in charge of Post-production on *The Debt/La Deuda Interna* (Miguel Pereira 1988).

Duncan Petrie Research Officer at the BFI. His first book, *Creativity and Constraint in the British Film Industry*, was published by Macmillan in 1991.

Felix De Rooy Born in Curaçao, he studied painting and graphic art at the Vrije Akademie Psychopolis in The Hague and then film at New York University. In 1976 he founded the artists' collective 'Cosmic Illusion'. Films: *Désirée* 1984, *Almacita di Desolato* 1986, *Ava y Gabriel, Un Historia di Amor* 1990.

FOREWORD

Colin MacCabe

In June of 1989 the British Film Institute, at the behest of the then newly installed director Wilf Stevenson, set up a Research Division which brought together the existing departments of publishing, periodicals, education and television. The aim was to focus the Institute's existing efforts in order not only to improve them individually but also to make more explicit the task of intellectual innovation. Despite playing a crucial role in the development of the study of the moving image from the 60s onwards, the BFI's relationship to the production of new ideas had been somewhat haphazard and was largely a response to demands posed by others. While continuing productively to exploit the haphazard and improve its response to external suggestions, the Institute's ambition was to create a new kind of research organisation in which the development of ideas about the media would be intimately linked to their dissemination. From the beginning, questions of European media and their relation to new forms of European and old forms of national identity were placed at the top of the agenda. It was thus wholly appropriate that the first major conference at the NFT which utilised all the new division's resources was on the theme of European identity. By a happy coincidence the event, in June 1991, was also able to premiere the BFI's latest feature *Young Soul Rebels* which had just won the Critic's Prize at Cannes.

It was felt that the event was so successful that its proceedings warranted publication as the first volume of BFI Working Papers. The Working Papers are an integral part of the research initiative, intended to provide an occasional form of publication in which the fruits of the Institute's research can be presented in a form which is both solid yet provisional. It is hoped that this first volume will prove as fertile for its readers as the original conference did for its participants. The success of both are due largely to the incredible energy and tenacity of Duncan Petrie, while among other BFI staff who contributed to the success of the conference, Esther Johnson, Tana Wollen and Jacintha Cusack demand acknowledgment.

ACKNOWLEDGMENTS

Grateful thanks to all of those who contributed to this volume. I would also like to thank Esther Johnson and Jacintha Cusack for their invaluable help in the organisation of the *Screening Europe* Conference which gave rise to this volume, to Roma Gibson and Ron Hawkins for their editorial advice, and to Tana Wollen for her generous encouragement and guidance through both the organisation of the conference and the editing of this volume.

Duncan Petrie

INTRODUCTION

Change and Cinematic Representation in Modern Europe

Duncan Petrie

Europe is currently undergoing massive social and political change. Shaped by the legacies of colonialism, the collapse of Soviet-supported regimes in the East and the development towards greater economic and political integration in the West, the continent is a seething pot of cultural, national, regional, racial, political, religious and social diversity. Yet the idea of Europe still has some meaning as a unifying concept: 'Europe is present everywhere and yet invisible; the circumference is everywhere and the centre nowhere.'[1]

The major cultural crisis facing Europe is precisely the manner in which the idea of 'European identity' has been maintained in opposition to the underlying diversity and heterogeneity. This identity reflects an 'imagined' community, in Benedict Anderson's sense,[2] of a Europe which posits an essentialist cultural tradition rooted in Judeo-Christian religion, Roman law, Greek ideas on politics, philosophy, art and science, and all refracted through the Renaissance and the Enlightenment. This tradition, as Jan Nederveen Pieterse points out, promotes itself as being characterised by ideas of high culture, autonomy and liberty, and is frequently contrasted with the cultural traditions of 'others', be they Asia, Africa (both seen as uncultured or barbaric) or, in more recent times, America (which is characterised by crass populism). Such a conception conveniently overlooks both the diverse reality of cultural forms and cultural differences within Europe (both past and present), and the fact that it was this very European tradition which in the twentieth century generated both fascism and totalitarianism.[3]

In a Europe no longer divided by the Iron Curtain, no longer certain where it begins and ends, the search for identity and belonging becomes increasingly pertinent. David Morley and Kevin Robins explore this question of European identity in relation to the concept of 'Heimat' or home/land, debates opened up in Germany by Edgar Reisz's film *Heimat*. While the concept was developed in relation to the nation-state, it can also be applied to the wider continental context

1

in terms of underlying cultural connections which presumably must exist in the minds of some if the concept of a united Europe is to have any meaning beyond a simple federation of trading partners. Yet, as Morely and Robins point out, this Utopian search is rather ominous in that it is about

> conserving the 'fundamentals' of culture and identity. And, as such, it is about sustaining cultural boundaries and boundedness. To belong in this way is to protect exclusive, and therefore, excluding, identities against those who are seen as aliens and 'foreigners'. The 'other' is always and continuously a threat to the security and integrity of those who share a common home.[4]

The notion of 'Heimat' is rooted in a lost and largely mythical past, blind to the fact that cultural essentialism is a falsehood. It finds expression in Britain through the explosion in the 1980s of the heritage industry, a celebration of Englishness and traditional values. The cinematic and televisual versions of this phenomenon are the numerous adaptations of writers such as E. M. Forster and Evelyn Waugh which, while often attempting to be critical, tend to fetishise the past by means of sumptuous visual style and production design, and which view that past (often sympathetically) from the perspective of a class threatened by social change and the dissolution of traditional rigid barriers. As Cairns Craig notes, the popularity of films like *A Room with a View, A Handful of Dust, Maurice* and *Where Angels Fear to Tread* 'is symptomatic of the crisis of identity through which England passed during the Thatcher years'.[5]

'Heimat' blatantly ignores the multicultural realities of many modern European societies. Members of society who do not fit the heterosexual, white, Anglo-Saxon, Christian credentials of the 'European' citizen are inevitably constructed as alien 'others', at best to be tolerated, at worst persecuted and subjugated. This perspective also misses the crucial point that culture and cultural identities are always in a state of flux, never static or given. They are constantly subject to development, transformation and change. This is analogous to Marshall Berman's conception of modernity which he describes as 'a unity of disunity': 'To be modern is to be part of a universe in which, as Marx said, "all that is solid melts into air".'[6] The impact of the European colonial heritage and the waves of economic migrancy encouraged by advanced capitalism has served to intensify these processes.

The fear of the 'other' generated by the search for European identity

2

also has an external dimension. This underpins the image of 'Fortress Europe', a united Europe under threat from outside (in particular from the Middle East and North Africa). As the 'Red threat' posed by the Soviet Union has receded with the thawing of the cold war so we have seen the spectre of Islamic fundamentalism rise to the top of the hierarchy in Western demonology. Pieterse points out that, 'as internal borders become lower, the external borders become higher, both in terms of ... the internal market and in terms of "European identity" '.[7] Immigration becomes subject to increasingly harsh and restrictive regulation.

These cultural and social issues have occupied the work of filmmakers in Europe who have, in a multitude of ways, grappled with the complexities of contemporary European identity (more productively, and accurately, recast as identities in Europe), examined the relationship between present and past, given cultural expression to voices which had previously been marginalised or silenced, and reflected and commented on the processes of social change and cultural transformation as they are worked out in a European context.

While all forms of cultural production have a role to play in the reconstruction of identity in Europe, the production of audovisual fictions can occupy a particularly significant position in this process. The creation of images is a complex process of making visible, of forcing an audience to look, to question and to reassess the nature of the world around them. Consequently, the medium of cinema provides a unique means by which the cultural heterogeneity, diversity and richness characterising modern Europe can be rendered visible and cultural essentialism unmasked as a dangerous and reactionary fallacy. Cinema can help us to recognise the complexities of identity, including processes of transformation and change.

But cinema cannot just be reduced to a simple reflection of some external concrete 'reality'. It can also interrogate the more subjective and inaccessible realms of identity, such as questions of desire (and the negative and destructive consequences of repressed desire) and fantasy. In contemporary society the power of the image is such that the audiovisual media play a fundamental role in the actual construction of realities. It is through images that most of us learn to understand and comprehend the world and ourselves. Furthermore, we are talking about a realm of the imaginary where not only are old identities interrogated, deconstructed and in some cases discarded, but new identities, new images and new social possibilities are being created and played out. If identity formation is in a constant state of becoming, as at least one of the commentators in this volume argues, then the image is central to the working through of this complex process.

Yet such arguments are rather Utopian in the sense that the mere

3

production of images (a problematic enough task in itself, given the economic resources required to make a film in the first place) is not enough. Structures must exist which make it possible for images to be seen by audiences. Images can also be used to reinforce tradition and orthodoxy, to reassure rather than confront. This, by and large, is the project of most mainstream cinema, be it American, British, French or whatever. The more radical and controversial the images, the more difficult it becomes to gain access to the distribution and exhibition networks and to find an audience. This is the dilemma faced by film-makers who want to confront key questions of the politics of identity and culture in contemporary Europe.

The major intentions of the 'Screening Europe' Conference held at the National Film Theatre in London on 7–8 June 1991 were to focus on these questions of European identity and audiovisual culture. The organisers decided to invite a range of academics and film-makers to discuss these issues, and a series of films were chosen to provide a context, a set of common reference points to which both speakers and audience would have access. It was also hoped that this arrangement would help to contain the discussion which, by virtue of the topic in hand, promised to be rather far-reaching and eclectic. The films chosen (not definitive by any standard, but significant nevertheless) were Derek Jarman's *The Tempest* and Jean-Luc Godard's *Passion*, both of which raise questions of the old, essentialist European cultural traditions of colonialism and high culture respectively; Claire Denis's *Chocolat*, a meditation on the French experience of colonialism; Pedro Almodóvar's *Women on the Verge of a Nervous Breakdown*, an example of popular contemporary European film-making which force-fully demonstrates how Spain has changed since Franco and is an example of a European film currently being remade by Hollywood; Emir Kusturica's *Time of the Gypsies*, an ironic commentary on migrancy and social and economic divisions in southern Europe; and Isaac Julien's *Young Soul Rebels*, a film which tackles questions of cultural, racial and sexual heterogeneity within a specifically British framework. These films (with the exception of *Young Soul Rebels*, which was seen by the public for the first time on the Friday night of the conference) were all screened at the NFT in the week leading up to the main event. (Credits and plot synopses of these films are included in the appendix.)

The work done at this conference was subsequently developed and complemented by the 1991 BFI Summer Conference, organised by the BFI's Education Department and held at Stirling University from 27 July to 2 August. This conference, entitled 'Borderlines: Films in Europe', examined the role and status of cinema in Europe in a variety of contexts, both historical and contemporary. The historical part exam-

4

ined the formation of 'national cinemas' in Italy, France and Germany, the contemporary explored questions of nation, identity and difference, focusing on differently located and self-locating marginal groups within Europe. The films screened and the questions and issues generated in this section of the conference provided an interesting supplement to the proceedings at 'Screening Europe', broadening the scope of the debate still further, and so merits a brief consideration here.

The issue of marginality was explored from three separate filmic perspectives: the Celtic peripheries of the United Kingdom, in particular Scotland and Northern Ireland, the predicament of North African immigrants in France (so-called 'Cinéma Beur'), and the plight of the Romany community in southern Europe, explored through *Time of the Gypsies*. The debates around the Celtic fringe were anchored by screenings of two very different films in terms of their formal construction and thematic preoccupations.

Timothy Neat and John Berger's *Play Me Something* draws connections between differently located contemporary experience on the peripheries of Europe – the Scottish Hebrides and the Dolomite mountains in northern Italy – through the medium of storytelling. What is interesting is that, in connecting a Scottish experience to a continental experience, the film bypasses any reference to England or to London. Philip Schlesinger notes that the film brings the rural settings of Italy and Scotland together into a common European frame.[8] In this way, peripheral identities, far removed from the image of the modern European one imagines lies in the minds of EC bureaucrats, are explored through an explicitly European perspective which successfully holds together issues of unity and difference.

The second film examined was *Hush a Bye Baby*, a production of the Derry Film and Video Collective in Northern Ireland, directed by Molly Harkin. This film charts the anguish of a Derry teenager who finds herself pregnant in a community which, as Martin McLoone puts it, 'values the sanctity of conception above the rights of the mother while at the same time frowning upon pregnancy outside the sanction of marriage'.[9] What is interesting about the film is its ambivalence towards constructions of an Irish identity forged in opposition to British oppression (vividly signified by the presence of troops on the streets of Derry and the internment of the heroine's boyfriend). *Hush a Bye Baby* draws parallels between the external oppression of the British state and the internal oppression of an Irish culture welded to Catholic dogma. The film tackles head-on the contradictions of 'Irishness', forged in resistance to colonisation and yet in some ways less progressive than the culture of the coloniser. The predicament of the girl is far less oppressive under the liberal legislation of the British state than that of the Ireland she regards as her country. As McLoone argues, 'it is the very richness of the dominant culture which poses a dilemma for peripheral nation-building in the first place'.[10]

The challenge for cultures which find themselves such victims of history (Scotland is another example) is to resist falling into the trap of the old nationalist dictum that it is better to live in the backward ignorance of one's own culture than to live with progressive ideas imposed from outside. The dilemma of an identity forged in the face of external oppression is how to maintain a degree of self-criticism when all negativity is projected, almost by definition, on to the oppressive 'other'.

The examination of Beur cinema in France also proved to be extremely interesting and productive in the light of wider questions of European identity. In some ways Beur cinema is analogous to Black British cinema in that it allows the articulation of voices challenging essentialist constructions of national and cultural identity. Yet the North African community in France have their own specificities and experiences which in other ways make them very different from British residents of Afro-Caribbean origin. What is worth considering here is that in both cases we are actually talking about a small body of work, often very diverse, which tends to be subjected to a critical homogenisation. While politically there is strength in unity for groups beginning to forge representations of themselves, this can often efface the diversity not only of the works but also the experiences of the communities in question (a recasting of the dilemma of discussing European identity!).

The two examples of Beur cinema considered at the 'Borderlines' conference bear this out. Mehdi Charef's *Le Thé au harem d'Archimède* is set in the milieu of a depressed housing estate in the Parisian suburbs. Although the leading character Madjid is North African, the general thrust of the film demonstrates the similar (impoverished and brutalised) existence of Arab immigrant and French underclass alike. Indeed, it can be argued that the major social caveats in the film are as much about class, or even sex (the women have a particularly hard time in this film, being either mothers or whores) than about race. There is also an interesting generational difference in that while to all intents and purposes Madjid's life and experience are the same as those of his French buddy Pat, his mother sees him as an Arab. She is vehemently against him dating French girls or applying for French nationality. She also suggests that he returns 'home' to join the army as an alternative to the delinquent subculture he has found himself a part of in France.

This very scenario is explored in the second Beur film, *Cheb*, directed by Rachid Bouchareb. Merwan, the young Beur who has retained his Algerian nationality, is deported from France after committing a crime. He is forced to join the Algerian army but is unable to make friends or adapt to what in reality is for him a foreign culture and a foreign landscape. He cannot understand the language or the customs and is made to feel like an outsider. Merwan's predicament is given a different inflection through his girlfriend Malika who, despite having a French passport, has been effectively kidnapped by her family and taken back to Algeria. Yet, as she points out, this is a country which oppresses women. She is every inch the liberated Western woman who cannot come to terms with society 'back home'. Made since the rise of Jean-Marie Le Pen's popularity and beginning with a sequence of newsreel footage of riots and demonstrations against French oppression of Arab immigrants, *Cheb* forcefully demonstrates the dilemma of the Beurs – rejected by France yet unable to return to a culture which is alien to them.

This is, on the one hand, an exemplary post-colonial text (albeit one with a rather more pessimistic vision than, for example, *Young Soul Rebels*), which asks fundamental questions of identity and belonging: if Merwan and Malika are culturally 'French', then what does this say about French culture and what it means to be French in a post-colonial context? On the other hand, the film echoes earlier concerns in European art cinema of the existentialist dilemma of identity. In its relating of subject to landscape it recalls Antonioni's *The Passenger*. We find Merwan back in France, ironically in the French army (assuming the identity of a French soldier he meets in Algeria, this being the only way he can return). Indeed, this ending of the film ponders both the questions of existential crisis and the inability to escape one's fate which Antonioni explored through Jack Nicholson's reporter.

In different ways these films (*Play Me Something* perhaps to a lesser extent than the others) explore the dangers of cultural essentialism, rooted in the myth of 'Heimat' explored above. *Hush a Bye Baby* achieves this by way of the contradictory and complex relationship between core and periphery in the forging of national identity. *Le Thé au harem d'Archimède* and *Cheb* reflect the Arab dimension which is an indisputable part of contemporary French identity and French culture. The former demonstrates that the lived experience of French Arabs resident in France need not be experienced as contradictory: Madjid may be Arab but he is also undeniably French, and it is ridiculous for his mother to suggest he goes 'home' when is already home (the problematic explored in *Cheb*). Madjid's cultural competence is that of a French youth living on the margins of a delinquent subculture, and this is perhaps the rub. The onus is placed on France to recognise the multicultural realities of its modern society and to dismantle the structures of institutionalised racism which force immigrant families into the modern-day ghetto of the housing estate. The legacy of post-colonialism is this virtual transformation of cultural identity in the heartland of nineteenth-century imperialism. White Europe must come to terms with this legacy if it is not to disintegrate in sectarian, racial and religious strife.

An account of the 'Screening Europe' Conference proceedings follows, including an essay by Colin MacCabe which combines elements of his introduction to the conference with a closer consideration of the significance of the work of Derek Jarman in relation to the theme of the conference, papers by Ien Ang, John Caughie and Stuart Hall; a report on the panel of film-makers (Felix De Rooy, Isaac Julien, Claire Denis, Chantal Akerman and John Akomfrah); and transcripts of the final panel of respondents (Nancy Condee, Vladimir Padunov, Patrizia Lombardo and Fredric Jameson). The appendices include edited transcripts of Colin MacCabe's interview with Jean-Luc Godard which started the event, an article 'Mapping the European Mind', by Antoine Compagnon, who did not speak at the conference but was in attendance throughout, and the credits and synopses of the six films screened as part of the event.

Notes

1. Antoine Compagnon, 'Mapping the European Mind', published in this volume, see Appendix 2.
2. Benedict Anderson, *Imagined Communities* (London: Verso, 1983).
3. Jan Nederveen Pieterse, 'Fictions of Europe', in *Race and Class: Europe, Variations on a Theme of Racism* (London: Institute of Race Relations, 1991).
4. David Morley and Kevin Robbins, 'No Place like *Heimat*: Images of Home(land) in European Culture', in *New Formations*, no. 12, Winter 1990, pp. 2–3.
5. Cairns Craig, 'Rooms Without a View', *Sight and Sound*, June 1991.
6. Marshall Berman, *All that is Solid Melts into Air: The Experience of Modernity* (London: Verso, 1983), p. 15.
7. Pieterse, 'Fictions of Europe', p. 5.
8. Philip Schlesinger, 'Scotland, Europe and Identity', in Eddie Dick (ed.), *From Limelight to Satellite* (London: BFI/Scottish Film Council, 1990).
9. Martin McLoone: 'Lear's Fool and Goya's Dilemma', *Circa*, no. 50, March/April 1990.
10. Ibid.

A POST-NATIONAL EUROPEAN CINEMA

A Consideration of Derek Jarman's
The Tempest and *Edward II*

Colin MacCabe

In many ways an event on European cinema at the National Film Theatre is almost wearyingly familiar. On many occasions in the last five years the NFT has played host to discussions about European cinema, but what distinguished this conference from others is that its aim was to enquire whether there is or could be a European cinema. Behind that question is an even more basic query regarding the reality of European culture.[1]

In some senses it is almost impossible to question the notion of European culture; the two terms seem to necessarily define each other. But this definition of culture is specifically European: it relates to the great national cultures of Europe and to their founding fathers, the Dantes, Shakespeares and Goethes. But you only have to sit, as I have sat, in conferences on Europe with Europeans whose forebears come from the Caribbean or from the South Asian continent to realise how pointless such a litany can sound, how far removed those national cultures are from the contemporary realities of multinational and multi-ethnic Europe. The real question is, how are we to understand the founding moments of those great national cultures in conjunction with a Europe whose other founding moment has come back to haunt it? If we think back to that period in the sixteenth century when Western Europe expanded to asset-strip the globe, what comes back in the twentieth century is the fundamental asset of labour which is now imported to service late capitalism.

The problem is that if we wish to grasp the reality of this moment it becomes difficult to know, or to understand, how we can define it as specifically European. In the movement from the sixteenth to the twentieth century we pass from a European to a global perspective, a perspective which demands that we analyse contemporary culture in terms of an imperialist imposition of authoritative norms which are then contested, negotiated, mimicked in the crucial emphases of our post-modernity. But that post-modernity would seem to have no more

9

time for European than for national cultures as the crucial terms become the global and the local.

It might seem that we can short-circuit these theoretical difficulties by appealing to a practical political level at which European culture makes sense. Independently of the particular political rows about the single currency, or the powers of the European Commission, the European Community is becoming an ever-increasing political reality, and it is that political reality which is increasingly part of any European cultural agenda. It is such pragmatic realities which dominate much of our institutional concerns at the British Film Institute and have dominated the multitude of conferences on Europe which this theatre has hosted. And these concerns and conferences are not without their successes. The MEDIA 95 programme proliferates, growing new arms like a monster from a fifties sci-fi movie. But it is when one reflects on an initiative like MEDIA 95 that one realises that there is no real way to short-cut the theoretical problems by appeals to political reality. All the discussions around Media 95 make two massive cultural assumptions: the first is that American cinema is a cultural threat, and the second, as a necessary corollary, is that there is some evident meaning to the notion of European cinema and European culture. Within such forums any attempts to raise genuine questions about European culture are treated both as impertinent and irrelevant. Impertinent because we all know what European culture is, irrelevant because we must eschew such intellectual levity for the realistic rigours of 'policy'. In fact, almost all appeals to 'policy', like its repellent semantic cousin 'management', are appeals away from a reality which is too various and too demanding. But it is the cultural reality of Europe which must be faced, and faced urgently, if we are not to bungle the enormous possibilities offered by the growing movement towards political unification.

To understand our current cultural situation, it is my own deep belief that one must step into the 'dark backward abysm of time'. These are the words that Prospero uses at the beginning of The Tempest as he reveals to his daughter the world beyond their island. The world that we need to understand is not the Milanese court and its intrigues, which Prospero addresses, but the cultural space of the Elizabethan and Jacobean theatre which Prospero and Miranda inhabit. The film-maker who has been most preoccupied with this historical reality is Derek Jarman ever since, in Jubilee, the magus John Dee escorted Elizabeth I on a tour of her kingdom four hundred years on. For Jarman the investigation of what it is to be English is inseparable from a reworking of the controlling myths of the English Renaissance. Three years after Jubilee, Jarman made his own version of The Tempest.

Let us start with Shakespeare's version. The play starts eponymously with a tempest and a consequent shipwreck. The ship carrying the King of Naples back from the wedding of his daughter to an African (itself an interesting fact in the light of the play's concerns) is separated from its flotilla and wrecked on an island. The wreck itself divides the passengers and crew: Ferdinand, the heir, finds himself alone; the nobles form one group and the crew, with the exception of Trinculo, are confined to the ship and kept there for the duration of the play. It is at this point that we learn from Prospero, the magician who rules the island, the history of the island, or rather the history of his arrival and conquest of the island. He disposes of the former ruler of the island, the witch Sycorax, frees her captive Ariel, the airy spirit, who is then bound to him for twelve years (a period which will coincide with the end of the play), and enslaves her son Caliban, this 'thing of earth'. The play then pursues two sub-plots in which the nobles plot against the king and Caliban conspires with Trinculo to overthrow Prospero, while the main theme follows the courtship of Ferdinand and Miranda, all these events obsessively supervised by Prospero with the help of his spy Ariel.

While the play may seem entirely European, set in the Mediterranean, its source is not (as for almost all of Shakespeare's other work) a European story but a contemporary event in the Caribbean. In 1609, while sailing off Bermuda, an expedition led by Sir Thomas Gates was caught in a tempest, his ship was separated from the rest, and he was presumed lost. A year later Gates arrived in Virginia, having spent the intervening year on a magical island, which furnished the survivors with all they needed to eat and drink. It is from this contemporary story that Shakespeare actually weaves his tale. In this context it becomes clear that the problematic of *The Tempest* is the problematic of the relationship between Europe and the New World which had only been discovered a century before and was in the process of colonial appropriation. Caliban is not simply this 'thing of earth', the savage man who has a long history in European thought, but also an anagram of his own name: the cannibal, the inhabitant of this new world. Prospero's relationship with him is evidently, among other things, an allegory of Europe's relation with the New World.

It is fashionable at the moment, in the current jargon of postcoloniality, to read *The Tempest* entirely in relation to Caliban, to stress the extent to which one must understand the play as Shakespeare's meditation on the particular way in which the colonial is constituted as what is not civilised but then, in a complicated and reciprocal moment, is considered to be that which defines civilisation. In the contemporary critical climate this is defined as the political reading. From this point of view Jarman's *Tempest* is an embarass-

11

ment, for his Caliban is white and the concerns of colonialism are largely absent from his film. But these contemporary readings ignore another, and as important, political reading which concentrates on the formation of the new nation-states which will dominate global history for the next four centuries. Explicitly, these concerns are present in *The Tempest* in terms of the politics of the court of Milan. Jarman rigorously excludes all such concerns from his film.

In *The Tempest*, however, he makes clear how Prospero's reign is one of terror. It was, not that long ago, fashionable to imagine the Elizabethan age as one of social harmony. More recently, and in the wake of the new historicism, political divisions have been understood as contained by cultural power. What both ignore are the twin foundations of the Elizabethan terror state, torture and espionage. If one wants to think of London at that time then what I always think of first are the gates, the walls of the city, outside which are the theatres along with the brothels and the new factories, but mounted on which are the bleeding quarters of those who have just been executed – noted by contemporary Protestant tourists to London as signs of England's civilisation. The crucial element in this machinery of terror was Walsingham's secret service, and we can read Ariel in *The Tempest* as an allegory of that secret service, forced under pitiless conditions to spy on every corner of the island and to bring to his master Prospero that information which underpins his power. It is for this reason that Jarman's *Tempest* concentrates on the relationship between Prospero and Ariel with its barely supressed sexual undertones. Jarman's homosexuality is what leads him to concentrate on the repression at the heart of the English state from which all the other repressions follow. The complete containment of sexuality within sanctified heterosexual marriage, the rigorous policing of desire and excess, the focusing of male sexuality and the denial of female sexuality. These are the fundamental themes of *The Tempest*, the sexual politics which underpin the birth of capitalism as it appropriates its colonial surplus.

But Jarman clearly understands, even more clearly in his art than in his discourse, how this sexuality is linked to certain traditions of representation. For if the security apparatus is the skeleton of the state, then the new national culture is the flesh. At the heart of this culture is a rigorous divorce between representation and audience. The traditional, and much mocked, reading of *The Tempest* is that it is autobiographical, that Prospero is Shakespeare and that when Prospero at the end says that 'every third thought shall be my grave', it is Shakespeare's own voice that we should hear as he bids adieu to his audience. In fact, if that traditional autobiographical account is placed within the wider context of theatrical history then it once again becomes very plausible. The theatre in which Shakespeare started to

12

work at the beginning of the 1590s and in which Marlowe was already the transgressive star was a very different theatre from that to which he bid farewell in 1611. Not only was it more directly popular and addressed a much wider social audience but it was also one which posed direct political and cultural threats to the state. By the time he wrote *The Tempest*, Shakespeare was writing for a representational space which was much more contained both aesthetically and socially. That is the crucial point of the masque that Prospero puts on for the lovers in Act IV, the masque that will celebrate their wedding. In his instructions to Ferdinand and Miranda, his attempts to control them as they sit, his order that 'No tongue! all eyes! be silent,' Prospero reproduces the new relationship to the audience, a relationship where without tongues, reduced to vision, the audience is excluded from the representational space. It is this space, directly filiated to an aristocratic culture, which disinherits the popular traditions on which Shakespeare had drawn so contradictorily. The biographical nature of the farewell comes in the recognition of what has been repressed and disinherited.

It is the fracturing of that representational space which makes *The Tempest* such a subversive film, for it sets itself not on an island but in a ruined aristocratic house, an imperial monument. If the viewer grasps that this is a house, there is no way in which he or she can organise the space that is presented. We cannot connect room to room or inside to outside. And, as if to make the point even more explicit, Caliban is played by Jack Birkett, the blind actor. It is this Caliban's blindness which places him categorically outside Prospero's cultural space. But if we can understand Jarman's undoing of the space of *The Tempest*, if we can see him using the cinema to undo the rigid distinctions of culture and sexuality which *The Tempest* so brilliantly performs, we must also admit that, in many ways, and whatever the borrowings from the popular culture of the twentieth century, it remains caught within that exclusive cultural space that it seeks to undermine. Brecht's 'fundamental reproach' to the cinema was that it could never escape that divorce between representation and audience which he termed 'Aristotelian' but which is more properly understood in terms of the Renaissance theatre.

In the aftermath of *The Tempest*, one could be left wondering where this filmic subversion of the relation between representation and audience could ever do more than endlessly interrogate itself. Jarman's disruption of cinematic space (in terms of costumes, sets, and articulation of shots and scenes) seems to invite (like so many leftist critiques) a nostalgic Utopia in which the ideal is a carnivalesque union of audience and representation, a return to a moment before any of the divisions of labour on which capitalism constructs itself. That carnival is, of course, realised for Jarman in the super-8 films of the 70s, but they remain irredeemably private, films which can only be truly enjoyed (as in their original screenings) by an audience entirely composed of their actors.

The counterpart of this personal privacy is the absence of any real public political sphere in *The Tempest*. Jarman excises the power politics of the kingdoms of Naples and Milan, but the film is then left in a curious vacuum in which the critique of representation and sexuality remains curiously unanchored. Jarman triumphantly solves this problem in *Edward II* when the political plot is made to turn (and turn even more emphatically in Jarman's version than Marlowe's) on direct sexual repression. *Edward II* would seem to mark a final settling of accounts with Jarman's chosen historical space: that interface between the Renaissance and the present which was first unveiled by John Dee in *Jubilee* and which has been investigated again and again, in *The Tempest*, in *The Angelic Conversation*, in *Caravaggio*. But all these films fade into 'prentice works beside the achievement of *Edward*. Christopher Hobbs's sets and Sandy Powell's costumes triumphantly realise what one now sees was only hinted at in *Caravaggio* (and Italy may always have been a diversion): a world which is always both now and then (both twentieth and sixteenth century) but is always England. At its heart is the constitutive relation which founds the modern English state on a repressive security apparatus and a repressed homosexuality. Jarman makes all these arguments with the deftness and lightness of a painter's hand. From the moment that Mortimer appears with the dress and bearing of an SAS officer in Northern Ireland, the equations between past and present, between state and sexuality, are clearly visible on the screen.

Jarman's *Edward* continues a debate about national and sexual identity which goes back four centuries to that moment at the beginning of the 1590s when the Elizabethan stage became the privileged symbolic space for a whole society. The exact date of Marlowe's play might seem of interest only to the most pedantic of scholars but, in fact, it is crucial to the play's significance that it comes right at the end of Marlowe's career, probably in 1592. Crucial, both personally and culturally, for by 1592 Marlowe was a man deeply engaged not only with the Elizabethan theatre but also with that other alternative employment for a man of letters who did not want to join the church or to occupy the position of learned scholar in a great lord's house: he was deeply implicated in the modern foundations of the Elizabethan state – Walsingham's secret service.

Culturally the play can be seen as a direct response to Marlowe's new rival Shakespeare whose trilogy *Henry VI* had attempted to produce a version of English history which would find ethical and

14

political meaning in the bloody shambles which had produced the Tudor dynasty. Marlowe's response is that of the arrogant intellectual who has known the pleasures of both political and sexual transgression. There is no meaning to be deduced from these chronicles of blood and treachery, except Mortimer's wheel of fortune (a sixteenth-century version of Ford's dictum that 'History is bunk' but with none of that twentieth-century tycoon's optimism), and to emphasise the nihilism Marlowe places a perverse love at the centre of his story. But for Marlowe this perversity is very closely linked to the new learning from which he draws his own legitimacy. There is absolutely no warrant in the chronicles for turning Gaveston and Spenser into intellectual parvenus. Edward's minions they may have been, but they were as well born as Mortimer and the other barons. For Marlowe they represent the new class, of which he is a prominent member, who will sell their learning to the new state but will, in the end, be crushed by that very same state. It is Gaveston's and not Edward's death which uncannily foreshadows Marlowe's own end, that great reckoning in a small room when Ingram Frisar, almost certainly with the Privy Council's blessing, stabbed Marlowe days before he was to appear before that same Council to answer charges of blasphemy. Four hundred years on, Marlowe's death remains no less of a mystery but it is not unreasonable to speculate (as has become wearingly and repetitively obvious in our own century) that political and sexual secrets make the most likely of bedfellows and that in an age when sodomy was a capital offence there may have been more than one member of the Council who was concerned that Marlowe's testimony might end with a lethal outing.

Jarman's film is not, however, Marlowe's play. Marlowe's identification with new knowledge and learning of the Renaissance gets no response from the director ('such an intellectual queen', as Jarman remarks in a marginal note to the script), and Derek's Gaveston and Spenser are not overlearned smart young men working for MI5 but very rough trade indeed. What Jarman has always insisted on is that he be recognised for what he is, and *Edward II* is, in that sense, unquestionably his most autobiographical work in what has been a consistently autobiographical *oeuvre*. But it is the bovine, middle-class ox Edward that Jarman identifies with, not the street-smart Gaveston whom he loves but who is here presented without redeeming feature except that 'he loves me more than all the world'. The film is also much more unambiguous in its misogyny than ever before. In that gay dialectic where identification with the position of the woman is set against rejection of the woman's body, *Edward II* is entirely, and without any textual foundation, on the side of rejection. For Marlowe, as for his age, the love of boys is merely the ultimate sexual transgression, not in any sense an alternative to heterosexual sex. It is here that

15

Jarman does violence to his source, making Edward's passion for Gaveston a consequence of his inability to be roused by the queen's body, a truly chilling scene at the beginning of the film. This is itself horribly overtrumped at the end, however, by the murder of Kent when Tilda Swinton's magnificent Isabella literally tears the life out of him with her teeth; every fantasy of the castrating woman, the *vagina dentata*, rendered into all too palpable image.

But there is love in this film, and a love which redeems history. The film is punctuated by scenes from the end of the play as Edward and his murderer-to-be, Lightborn, discourse in the bowels of the castle where the king is imprisoned. We await throughout the film the fabled end, the vicious poker which will leave a king dead and humiliated and without a mark on him. It is this end that the film has prepared us for as we see the homophobia which courses as a vicious lifeblood through our history and our culture. No fault of Gaveston's can possibly excuse or justify the hatred which is spat out at him as he is forced through a gauntlet of hatred on his way to exile and a death unbearable in its explosion of destructive violence. As Mortimer comes to upbraid the king for his moral turpitude, the barons at his back suddenly reveal themselves as a moral majority stretching back and forth across the centuries, an endless, and endlessly unpleasant, Festival of Light.

But after the end that Marlowe and history has prepared us for, Jarman has contrived a happy end from the resources of his own fight against death. As Lightborn approaches the king for a second time with the dreaded poker in his hand, it falls from his hands and in a moment of real tenderness he bends and kisses the king. With this kiss a whole history of homophobia and violence is annulled, a whole new history becomes possible.

It is at this point that *Edward II* becomes possible, drawing the audience into the most private of worlds, not merely as spectator but as participant (and in this respect the published screenplay is an integral part of the film). The Outrage slogans which punctuate the text, like the film itself, demand reaction. It is in the multiplication of the forms of address around the text that Jarman provides a solution to Brecht's 'fundamental reproach'. For Brecht, the theatrical setting is still a unity, the alienation devices simply fragment that unity from within. Jarman, here working with the grain of advanced capitalism, breaks the unity of the cinema experience from without. The celebrity interview, that crucial tool of marketing, is here turned into a method of disrupting any separation of public and private, and thus depriving the moment of viewing of any simple aesthetic unity.

It is this multiplication of address, and its refusal of the divorce between public and private, which enables Jarman to solve the problems of *The Tempest* in *Edward II*. The private is made public and, as a result, the public sphere can be incorporated into the film. The state, which disappears from his *Tempest*, is now centre stage but that stage can also be the most public proponents of the abolition of privacy, the militants of Outrage. It is not, I think, unreasonable to suggest that it is the pressure of death, that unique meeting of the public and private, that has been the catalyst for the extraordinary experiments that have marked the last five years of Jarman's work. This is signalled within the film itself when, as the screen dims, the final lines, which are Jarman's rather than Edward's or Marlowe's, are:

Come death, and with thy fingers close my eyes,
Or if I live let me forget myself.

It is striking at this point, and in the context of the politics of any future European film, to compare Jarman's film with Branagh's *Henry V*. *Henry V* is a crucial play for Shakespeare – both the final answer to the problems that Marlowe had posed him seven years earlier in *Edward II* and the first play in the new Globe theatre. The power politics with which the bishops open the play is transcended by the national divinity which Henry represents. And the final farewell to an older cultural space is witnessed in the death of Falstaff, standing in for Will Kemp's (the great clown who had embodied Falstaff) refusal to join the new company. It can come as a surprise only to those who refuse to understand the links between sexuality and representation that it is in this play that the formal mastering of the female body is accomplished by the naming of Katherine's body in English and her marriage to the English king. It says a lot about the sheer bad taste of Branagh's film that his idea of taking licence with the text is to have Falstaff appear in flashback and to rehearse the famous Chimes at Midnight speech (which only makes sense as a conversation between two old men) as a dialogue between Hal and Falstaff. But this is all of a piece with the cultural nostalgia of Branagh's project (which is exactly captured in the name of his company). The Renaissance theatre will now use the cinema to reproduce the Elizabethan stage shorn of all its contradictions. What in Olivier's magnificent film is the cultural corollary of the last tragic moment of the English state (extinguishing its own empire in the fight against Fascist Germany) becomes in Branagh's tepid offering the farcical analogue of Thatcher's hideous mimicry of Churchill. Jarman's use of his Renaissance model has absolutely nothing to do with Branagh's. *Edward II* (as in Olivier's *Henry V*) is placed at the service of pressing contemporary concerns. Unlike Olivier, however, Jarman's film responds to

17

both public and private need and calls the very distinction into question.

I think that these reflections should enable us to understand something of the specificity of European film. What is specific to Europe, within a global context which emphasises the local and the international, is the question of the nation-state. It is no accident that Jarman never hesitates to stress his cultural conservatism, for what he returns to, again and again, are the founding myths of Englishness. Jarman, it could be argued, is trying to rescue, from underneath the monument of the nation, the last ethnic minority – the English. It is exactly the release of these buried ethnicities which constitutes the reality and risks of European culture and politics today. This is not to say that there is no question of cultural prescriptivism, that all European film-makers should now address the question of the nation. What it does say is that in so far that European film-makers make films that are specifically European, those films will focus on the reality of national identities and the possibilities that are contained in their transgression.

Notes

1. All papers from conferences enjoy the virtues of hindsight. This paper is substantially different from that delivered at the conference because I was able to see the finished *Edward II* some ten days after the conference. In the talk I delivered I anticipated that *Edward II* would move the debate on. It did, in ways that I have tried to reflect in this version. An earlier and shorter version was published in the October number of *Sight and Sound* under the title 'Throne of Blood'.

SCREENING EUROPE: IMAGES OF POST-COLONIALISM

A Conference at the National Film Theatre
7–8 June 1991

EVENT TIMETABLE

FRIDAY 7 JUNE 1991
7.00 p.m. Welcome and Introduction by Colin MacCabe
7.30 p.m. Jean-Luc Godard in conversation with Colin MacCabe
9.30 p.m. Screening of *Young Soul Rebels*

SATURDAY 8 JUNE 1991
10.00 a.m. Papers presented by:
　　　　　Ien Ang, John Caughie, Stuart Hall

　　　　　Chair: Philip Dodd

　　　　　Discussion

2.00 p.m. Film-makers Panel: Felix De Rooy, Isaac Julien,
　　　　　Claire Denis, Chantal Akerman, John Akomfrah

　　　　　Chair: Duncan Petrie

4.00 p.m. Final Panel of Respondents: Nancy Condee,
　　　　　Vladimir Padunov, Patrizia Lombardo, Fredric Jameson

　　　　　Chair: Colin MacCabe

Conference Organisers: Duncan Petrie, Jacintha Cusack,
　　　　　　　　　　　　Esther Johnson

SATURDAY MORNING SESSION
Introduction

Philip Dodd

I'm not quite sure whether we're at a funeral or a birth in having this conference – in other words, whether what we are talking about is the death of an old kind of Europe or the birth of a new one. It was Hegel who said that the owl of history only flies at dusk; and if that's the case, then the obsession with Europe may be precisely because at least one idea of Europe is dying. Nevertheless, if you look back over the last two hundred years of European history, you can excavate the ways the idea of Europe has been variously constituted through history.

I read Kenneth Clark's *Civilisation* the other week and it's fascinating to notice that Clark effectively excludes Spain from Europe on the grounds that it's simply barbarous. So it's well worth thinking that Europe is constituted not only on ethnic and racial grounds, which I suppose bears most heavily on us now, but also in terms of nation-states. And in those terms, if we are breaking from an idea of Europe, are we talking about new European identities or are we talking about new identities in Europe? I think that distinction is worth pondering. It may be that we should no longer think of Buñuel's *Un Chien Andalou* as a European movie but rather as part of Catalan modernism. On the other hand, if we are talking about new identities in Europe, it's also perfectly clear to me that that doesn't mean you can simply shuffle off the past, because those dead generations do weigh like a nightmare upon the brains of the living. And it seems that in some real way the discussion today not only has to come to terms with what is happening now, but also with what has happened in the past.

HEGEMONY-IN-TROUBLE

Nostalgia and the Ideology of the Impossible in European Cinema

Ien Ang

Europe can no longer be understood by starting out from Europe itself.
Jean Baudrillard

Baudrillard's *Amérique* is in fact, at least in part, a book about Europe. After two and a half months of travelling through the vastness of America, the French philosopher started brooding about what is often offhandly called the Continent (with a big C). He notes on his return that:

> What strikes you immediately in Paris is that you are in the nineteenth century. Coming from Los Angeles, you land back in the 1800s. Every country bears a sort of historical predestination, which almost definitively determines its characteristics. For us, it is the bourgeois model of 1789 – and the interminable decadence of that model – that shapes our landscape. There is nothing we can do about it: everything here revolves around the nineteenth-century bourgeois dream.[1]

A sense of the fatal, of radical fatalism, runs through the bulk of Baudrillard's work, so it is not surprising that he evokes here a sense of inevitability, the inevitability of predestination, in Europe's contemporary condition, as being haunted by the grandiose dreams of its own past. Baudrillard's claim that France is condemned to live its present in the shadow of the dreams of the French Revolution is an apt diagnosis for the contradictions of a typically European structure of feeling. It is the structure of feeling of the Old World, characterised by smug complacency on the one hand and by unrecognised nostalgia on the other. In fact, the two tendencies go so well together that Europeans derive a profound sense of self-confident, undoubting comfort from it. And it is a structure of feeling, I am afraid, that makes contemporary Europe rather ill prepared for the cultural renewal that is needed to come to terms with its changed position in the world. As with all

21

change, it has to begin with an altered sense of self. So the question to be raised is how Europe can start redefining its historically sedimented 'identity' and its habits of thought and action.

Surely, being European is neither a fixed nor a homogeneous thing; it means something different in different parts of Europe and at different moments of Europe's heterogeneous histories. Talk about 'Europe' as if it were a single entity is therefore deeply problematic, not only for reasons of the obvious internal diversity and conflict that rifts the continent in many different ways, but also because of the ideological and political significance of 'Europeanness' in world history. Still, it is precisely the promotion of such unified and renovated Europeanness which seems to be implied and strived for in the construction of the European Single Market in 1992, and culturally articulated in hegemonic media endeavours such as the late Robert Maxwell's newspaper *The European*. There is no doubt, then, that the forging of a new, pan-European identity suited to the economic and political necessities of the twenty-first century, 'a common European home' in Mikhail Gorbachev's phrase, is invested with considerable desire in official European culture today. However, it is clear that such a project is bound to be contradictory and full of conflicts.

Or to put it differently: what are we to make of the current obsession with 'Europe' among Europeans themselves? What is Europe's place in today's world? After all, the idea of Europe as more than just the name to describe a geographical region (whose boundaries towards the East are uncertain anyway), but as a cultural unity with moral superiority and rational supremacy, has underpinned the legitimacy of universal European dominance throughout the world in the modern period.[2] So, European power and authority, however benign and in the spirit of whatever 'new world order', can never be reasserted innocently, given the legacy of European colonialism and imperialism which inaugurated the emergence of today's thoroughly interdependent but unequal world system in the first place.[3] It is therefore important to address the issue of 'post-colonialism' in any discussion about the contours of a politically viable European 'identity' of the future.[4]

I was asked to shed light on these questions through a discussion of a number of European films of the 80s, among others Pedro Almodóvar's *Mujeres al borde de un ataque de nervios*, Jean-Luc Godard's *Passion*, Claire Denis's *Chocolat* and Emir Kusturica's *Time of the Gypsies*. (I have decided to leave Jarman's *The Tempest* out of my considerations here because I find the film quite unwatchable, not only for formalist reasons but also because I lack the cultural capital which is such a taken-for-granted part of Britishness: Shakespeare. A reminder of the partiality of preferred traditions of Europeanisms!)

22

The conference organisers told me that 'in different ways these films pose questions of European identity and European cinematic expression'. Of course, the cultural politics of this particular selection and its framing is worth enquiring in itself. For example, we might wonder whether it is really the cinema which should be the focus of examination and intervention in the (re)construction of representations of Europe. Isn't television a much more relevant or salient site of cultural production in this respect, especially given recent developments in transborder satellite transmission across Europe and related policy ambitions (in the context of the preservation of the lofty European tradition of public service broadcasting) such as the promotion of European co-productions? This is also to raise the rather neglected issue of European audiences and their divisions and differentiations, that is, the issue of circulation and consumption of these screen images and how they are interpreted and appropriated in multiple contexts. Let us not dwell on these considerations, but stick rather to the conference's title, which asks us to query how these films shape European images of post-colonialism. Let me take this opportunity, then, to use these films as a starting-point to think about some of the peculiar difficulties of European identity today.

I am forced to think about these questions while being physically removed from European space, and the tyranny of distance imposed by temporarily being 'tucked away' (from a European perspective) in Australia works as a liberating force to clarify the relativeness, and specificity of these European concerns. In a time when the ruthless, levelling force of global capitalism is spawning to an ever more encompassing extent the establishment of a global *cultural* order, the politics of cultural identity, construed as the foregrounding and promotion of particular, local-bound senses of cultural distinctiveness and difference, has gained an unprecedented relevance and urgency all over the world. However, since identity cannot be constructed in a vacuum but can only be forged through the active demarcation of a self in relation to some other, identity politics everywhere draws into its mode of operation a necessarily comparative spirit. And in today's global culture, the West, and arguably European culture in particular, still constitutes the universal point of reference in relation to which others define themselves as particularities. To give a trivial example, even Australia's casual self-definition as 'Down Under' only makes sense in the context of acceptance of a Eurocentric cartography of the globe. On the other hand, most of my European friends have urged me to come back 'home' soon, declaring simply and categorically that Australia is just too far away, that is, beyond the European horizon. The 'centre' experiences distance differently than does the 'periphery'.

The legacy of colonialism and imperialism, then, grants that Europe is still considered, both inside and outside Europe itself, as the real and imagined cultural (if not economic) centre of the world, the norm of human civilisation, which has put other cultures and peoples in a relation of subordination to itself. But in both theory and practice there is a growing sense of self-confidence and assertion of cultural autonomy and self-determination among the previously colonised. Post-colonial forms of cultural expression and representation are emerging everywhere in the peripheries, defying and challenging the received standards and perspectives of the European centre.[5] It is this challenge that European hegemony is now facing up to, an embarrassing predicament in which 'Europe' inevitably finds itself in the position of the father whose law is being undermined.

Europe's predicament, in other words, is analogous to the predicament of men in the face of the challenge of feminism. In this respect, it is worth pointing at the excessively patriarchal nature of official European culture. In *The Great Museum*, a book on the representation of European history in Europe's monuments, Australian cultural critic Donald Horne observes that the legitimisation of male authority is one of the most persistent dominant values by which European greatness has been celebrated and commemorated.[6] With the exception of some virtuous female symbols such as the Virgin Mary and Jeanne d'Arc, or the use of the sexualised female image to represent an idea such as Liberty, women are simply excluded from Europe's official, high-cultural self-representation. There is, in short, a profoundly masculinist bias in the European public sphere, which was perpetuated and reinforced, not undercut, by the emancipatory bourgeois movement of the French Revolution which still, *pace* Baudrillard, decisively shapes contemporary European sensibility.[7]

This is not the place to examine the specificity of European patriarchy and the particular problems it poses for feminism in Europe.[8] Suffice it to note that it is no wonder that even in the 'post-feminist' era of today, European women are still on the verge of a nervous breakdown! Spanish director Pedro Almodóvar's film is quite double-hearted about female frustration: on the one hand giving ample space, if mockingly, to the acting-out of women's rage (invariably caused by machismo selfishness), but at the same time presenting female solidarity as utterly fragile and the last resort for women to regain self-respect in their resignation to their defeat and powerlessness. The one feminist character in the film runs off with the despised male anti-hero who gets away with all the heartache, despair and anger he caused in the first place. In the end, then, patriarchal masculinity is put on comic display here, only to leave male superiority somewhat bruised but ultimately untouched in the film's closure. In this sense, the very representation of the female 'other' as being 'on the verge of a nervous breakdown' can be seen as a masculinist strategy to accommodate and trivialise the critical challenge of feminism. The film's reassuring message is that patriarchal power relationships are impossible to overturn. As we shall see, as with patriarchy, so for Europe.

What, then, about Father Europe's response to the assault on its superiority? After all, in this post-colonial world, the European problem, much like the problem of male dominance, is the problem of dominance-in-distress, hegemony-in-trouble. In other words, while previously colonised peoples and cultures are constructing their present by struggling out of the derivative identities imposed upon them in the past, the Europeans are in a quite different predicament: they are logically forced to come to terms with their waning cultural hegemony and to redefine themselves accordingly, as particular rather than universal, as located rather than transcendental, specific rather than general.

However, the power-laden, exploitative cultural encounters of the past will not easily give way to an acceptance of cultural difference on equal terms. The task for Europe, then, is to stop relating to others by taking itself as the standard. Unfortunately (although I can only give a crudely simplified and perhaps unforgivingly generalised account here), the dominant tendency within European self-consciousness today is one which disavows rather than recognises this post-colonial circumstance. It seems to me that while Europe is now increasingly aware of its own particularity, this particularity tends to be defended and advanced in relation to the more recent global imperial powers, especially America[9] and, more recently, Japan. As a consequence, Europe's own colonialist and imperialist past, and its far-reaching cultural impact on the peoples and cultures subjugated under its rule, remains relatively unaddressed, and Europe's 'guilt' largely unprocessed. Consider, for example, French Minister of Culture Jack Lang's well-known tirade against the threat posed by American cultural imperialism to European audiovisual culture, which was expressed in a tone utterly confident about the absolute value of the latter and totally oblivious of Europe's own long history as a cultural imperialist.

Europe's impotence in productively dealing with its colonialist past can be highlighted through a reading of Claire Denis's film *Chocolat*. *Chocolat* recalls the last years of French West African colonialism through the memory of a young white woman, whose name is, significantly enough, France, and who in the late 1950s grew up as the daughter of a French district officer in Cameroon. The film is about the subjective *experience* of colonialism from both the perspective of the colonised, personified by the family's black servant Protée, and that of the little girl who was too young to understand what colonial power was about and who treated Protée as both her friend and her subordinate. For reasons that need not be explicated here the uneasy bond between the two ended abruptly, and incomprehensibly to France, almost coinciding with the end of the colonial period. When France returns to Cameroon many year later, in the 1980s, she finds herself unable to recover her colonial childhood; she'd like to see the house her family lived in, but isn't sure whether she should. Protée does not reappear.[10]

The film, then, problematises the difficulty, if not impossibility, of an unproblematic post-colonial re-encounter (and reconciliation) between coloniser and colonised, because those who were colonised have changed, no longer defining themselves in terms of dependency and marginalisation, no longer in silent, private and impotent wrath and suppressed desire as was the overtly loyal Protée, but busy transforming the colonial legacy into an emergent, self-determined identity, a society of their own. In fact, what France, or *France*, must realise is the ultimate *irrelevance* of her presence in this post-colonial African place: none of the locals pays any attention to her, she talks to no one, remains a bystander, an invisible onlooker. The only 'other' she teams up with is an African-American who came to Africa in the hope of rejoining his 'brothers' but finds that his identity is American, not African. 'They've no use of my being here. Here I am nothing, a fantasy,' he says. *His own* fantasy, we might add, just as France finds her past to have disappeared, unrecuperable – meaning (so the film suggests by emphasising France's detached silence) that she has no identity, reduced to nothingness. 'No past, no future.'

As a (provisional) ending, this lonely present held in timeless suspension is troublesome. If *Chocolat* can be read as a recognition of European inability to come to terms with its own colonialist record, it does so without offering us a way out of the repressed crisis of identity which remains so unacknowledged in the larger European context. The black American apparently has an easier job: his sense of meaning and purpose would be regained once he recognised America as his site of struggle for emergent identity.[11] For the white European, however, it is all too easy to be overwhelmed by a redemptive but unproductive sense of loss, to cling to a residual identity and be stuck in it because it is so comforting. To be sure, it is precisely a celebration of such a sense of loss, stripped of its historical particularity and unversalised in terms of the predicament of the modern human condition, which we encounter all too often in European audiovisual culture. We only have to think of Bertolucci's *The Sheltering Sky*, which uses an offensively aestheticising, orientalist representation of the non-Western 'other' as an alibi to focus in on the self-indulgent, tormented and unsuccessful search for meaning on the part of a bunch of individuals of European descent.

26

It is in the nature of hegemony to take its authority and universal validity for granted; a hegemony-in-trouble therefore tends to seek refuge in a set of defence mechanisms acting as modes of denial of its own creeping marginalisation. It may be a perverse leap of argument, but perhaps this is the very reason why Europe persists in living in the nineteenth century, as Baudrillard noticed after returning from the New World. This was the high period of European hegemony, sustained and legitimated by the progressivist, modernist values of post-French Revolution, post-Enlightenment bourgeois capitalism. Large parts of European self-understanding still seem to be dominated by a particularly strong faith in the universalist claims of the project of modernity which, according to Habermas, a quintessentially European thinker, remains uncompleted.[12] What is important to note, however, is not that Europeanist modernity is uncompleted but that it proves to be increasingly *uncompleteable* as a result of the waning of European hegemony.

It is in this sense that we can understand Baudrillard's claim that the crisis of Europe is 'a crisis of historical ideals facing up to the impossibility of their realisation'. If, as Fredric Jameson would have it, History is What Hurts, then what looms large in modern European historical consciousness are its failed Utopias: from the Enlightment to May 1968, from Empire to Thatcherism, from the Third Reich to German unification, from the dictatorship of the proletariat to *glasnost*. European modernity – social and philosophical, cultural and political – is driven by, and sets itself up through, a persistent, totalising longing for the impossible, perfect state, the perfect society. Even contemporary discourse on a United Europe is often invested with such high-minded Utopian overtones, even though the transcendental *Weltanschauung* underlying it is primarily a pragmatic one given the necessities of global capitalism today. But, as Baudrillard notes with a sense of weariness which in itself confirms the structure of feeling he discerns, 'Our (*sic*) problem is that our old goals – revolution, progress, freedom – will have evaporated before they were achieved, before they became reality. Hence our melancholy.'[13]

Godard's film *Passion* even radically *stages* this melancholic passion for the impossible: the impossibility of cinema itself, the impossibility of narrative, the impossibility of love, the impossibility of arriving at anything. A Polish film director, Jerzy, doesn't succeed in making a film which, significantly enough, attempts to recreate the scenarios of classic European paintings by Rembrandt, Goya, Delacroix and others in the form of tableaux vivants. He doesn't have a story, and his producer and crew are getting desperate. 'Is it because of what's happening in Poland?' they ask him. We don't get an answer. Poland in the early eighties, we should guess, was in the midst of upheaval led by Solidarnosc, the site of a passionate struggle for changing the present. But such passion, so concludes *Passion*, is no longer possible in contemporary France; all that's left is a passionate (but doomed) quest of passion itself. So there is no story to tell. 'You have to live stories before inventing them,' says Jerzy.

If this jaded posture can be seen as symptomatic for the present state of European self-consciousness, it explains why European cultural concerns are often so inward-looking, so self-enclosed, an implosion of a fetishistic, unbearable heaviness of being. Such melancholic longing for the impossible is an apology for self-centredness: it amounts to a naturalised sense of loss and the cultivation of nostalgia. It is not surprising that, of the films being discussed here, only *Mujeres*, which presents itself as a popular comedy (although even here the popular is self-consciously inflected with the formalist devices of modernist art: a genuinely *popular* European cinema seems to be an impossibility), manages to avoid the mood of nostalgic melancholy (but at an ideological cost, as we have seen), in contrast with the artistic minimalism of *Chocolat*'s narrative style and its moody ending.

In this respect, Europe's overdeveloped high culture, with its absolutist aestheticising tendency, may only exacerbate the problem. It is this tendency which tends to equate legitimate European cinema with art cinema (as evidenced by all the films discussed here), European television with 'quality' television. Art and quality – terms by which European culture promotes itself as absolute, identity which relegates all difference to the realm of the irrelevant (unless it can be appropriated within the categories of 'art' and 'quality'). However, this unchecked Eurocentrism obscures Europe's own increasing irrelevance in other regions of the world as the experience of colonialism retreats into memory.

The problem for Europe, then, is to learn how to marginalise itself, to see its present in its historical particularity and its *limitedness*, so that Europeans can start relating to cultural 'others' in new, more modest and dialogic ways. Godard's echoing of Lyotard's thesis that the period of grand narratives – that is, the period of hegemonic European modernity – is over should thus not lead to the conclusion that there are no longer stories to tell; on the contrary, it is the abandonment of the search for the universalising 'big story' which should open up the space for the telling of smaller, more particular stories. In the context of today's global interdependence, such stories carve out the possibility of insisting on the fact 'that every identity is placed, positioned, in a culture, a language, a history'.[14] At the same time, claiming that you no longer have stories to tell, as *Passion* suggests, is only a way of evading the confrontation with the limits of your own particularity; identity is thus made invisible, groundless,

28

generalised. It is for this reason that *Chocolat*'s ending is so disturbing. The film's emphasis on France's powerlessness in articulating her own, present, post-colonialist identity effectively neutralises the film's potentially enabling call for European self-interrogation. In the end, *Chocolat*, too, is a Eurocentric film.

That such self-interrogation is also important for Europe itself is clear. As most post-colonialist societies in Europe are becoming increasingly multicultural and multi-ethnic, an upshot (and a reminder) of the colonial past which cannot be denied or disregarded, a Europe that sees its culture as relative and permeable is essential if the narrowminded nationalism and petty racism that infects the continent is to be overcome. It is against this background, of course, that a film like *Time of the Gypsies* is significant. After all, the Gypsies are one of the oldest cultural 'others' within Europe's borders, a group of people whose inferior status has not changed for centuries, who have always been easily ostracised everywhere in Europe precisely because they do not form or belong to a 'nation'. If anything, Europe's treatment of the Gypsies only exemplifies the fundamental problems Europeans have with difference and otherness. In this sense, I am slightly concerned about the politics of *Time of the Gypsies*. To be sure, I found the film 'impressive', but even to use this word to describe the film's effect already marks a certain distance, a certain objectification. Although the film deals with the inside world of Gypsy life and experience, the film's magic realist aesthetics, thoroughly within the accepted codes of art cinema, might only serve to reinforce (for European audiences at least) the absolute 'otherness' of Gypsy culture, totally wrapped up in its own concerns and frustrations, outside modernity, forever condemned to remain at the fringes of mainstream Europe.

What, then, given this context, are the prospects for the future? Baudrillard, for one, is pessimistic: he too succumbs to the ideology of the impossible. 'Our European culture', he says, 'is one that has staked its all on the universal and the danger menacing it is that of perishing by the universal.'[15] But a pessimism of the intellect which duplicates itself in a pessimism of the will is bound to be vainly effete and impotent. A more positive gesture comes from Stuart Hall, who derives optimism from the empowering force of the very narratives of displacement which can be told by increasing numbers of exiles, expatriates and migrants who came to Europe from the ex-colonies – of all places! From here, Hall places hope in a new conception of 'ethnicity' which carries the beginning for a new politics of identity, one which not only insists on difference, specificity and conjuncture, but also on movement, articulation and syncretism. In other words, from this perspective Europe's hope for cultural renewal can paradoxically only come from those 'others' who came to Europe precisely as a result of

29

the history of European colonialism, such as Stuart Hall himself! And indeed, if we look at films like Frear's *My Beautiful Laundrette* and *Sammy and Rosie Get Laid*, Po Chih Leong's *Ping Pong* and, of course, Isaac Julien's *Young Soul Rebels*, we can see how they derive their vitality precisely from the necessity for and the pleasure of constant cultural *exchange* in the staking out of any 'identity'. It is also significant that none of these 'new ethnic' films, made in Europe but not from Europe, display the nostalgic melancholy that I have discussed earlier. These films attempt to come to terms with the complexities of the present without resorting to idealised images of either the past or the future; they are, in a sense, post-Utopian, fully aware of the fact that people living in Europe, while quite different from one another in interest, wealth, power, 'culture', are nevertheless, as Clifford Geertz has put it, 'contained in a world where, tumbled as they are into endless connection, it is increasingly difficult to get out of each other's way'.[16] What these films emphasise are not impossibilities, but the search for new possibilities. Perhaps, then, the best bet for Europe to disentangle itself from its hegemonic past is to become post-European.

Notes

This paper has benefited greatly from conversations with Jon Stratton, to whom my thanks.

1. Jean Baudrillard, *America* (London: Verso, 1988), p. 73.
2. See, e.g., Denys Hay, *Europe: The Emergence of an Idea* (Edinburgh: Edinburgh University Press, revised ed. 1968).
3. See Eric R. Wolf, *Europe and the People Without History* (Berkeley: University of California Press, 1982).
4. See Edward Said, 'Representing the Colonized: Anthropology's Interlocutors', *Critical Enquiry 15*, Winter 1989, pp. 205–25.
5. See, e.g., Bill Ashcroft, Gareth Griffiths and Helen Tiffin, *The Empire Writes Back* (London: Routledge, 1989).
6. Donald Horne, *The Great Museum* (London: Pluto Press, 1984).
7. See, e.g., Joan B. Landes, *Women and the Public Sphere in the Age of the French Revolution* (Ithaca and London: Cornell University Press, 1988).
8. One could think, for example, of the cultural specificity of the French feminisms of theorists such as Irigaray, Cixous and Kristeva for whom the feminine stands for the principle of what is repressed by the symbolic order of culture.
9. This tendency is particularly strong in the refined writings of Central European thinkers such as Gyorgy Konrad and Vaclav Havel. The post-Communist predicament, however, would need a separate examination.
10. The feminised name Protée for the black male servant may be seen as signifying the place to which the colonial 'other' is relegated in colonialist discourse: that of the diffuse feminine (see also footnote 9). According to

Claire Denis, director of the film, Protée was quite a common name used for black servants by French colonialists.

11. Of course America, or more precisely the United States, represents an altogether site for the struggle for cultural identity, which cannot be addressed here.
12. Jurgen Habermas, 'Modernity – an Incomplete Project', in Hal Foster (ed.), *Postmodern Culture* (London: Pluto Press, 1985).
13. Baudrillard, *America*, pp. 78–9.
14. Stuart Hall, 'Minimal Selves', *ICA Documents* 6 (London: ICA, 1987), p. 83.
15. Baudrillard, *America*, p. 83.
16. Clifford Geertz, *Works and Lives: The Anthropologist as Author* (Chicago: University of Chicago Press, 1988), p. 147.

BECOMING EUROPEAN
Art Cinema, Irony and Identity

John Caughie

Growing up, like an apparently increasing number of us, in the 1950s, before Continental holidays formed the familiar horizon of working-class or *petit-bourgeois* family leisure – before holidays themselves were a matter of everyday expectation – 'The Continent' (as it was called before Britain discovered Europe) was not a part of my generation's, or my class's, or my locality's extended playground. The characteristic holiday landscape was either coastal Butlins or, for me, West Highland caravan sites. My acquaintance with Europe began in 1962 with the student's hitchhiking Grand Tour (Paris, Nice, Florence, Venice, Geneva), but this was essentially a road movie, the object of the exercise being to cover distances vaster than were available in Britain rather than to discover the culture of our common European home. Just leaving school, still implacably romantic, I remember hitchhiking to Paris for the weekend; but this was an American pilgrimage – somebody had told us that we could sleep on the floor of the Paris bookshop where Henry Miller and Alan Ginsberg and William Burroughs had also slept. In 1967, newly graduated, I did the thing that was much more characteristic of my Scottish generation than European holidays: I emigrated to Canada. Coming at the tail end of a massive post-war emigration from Scotland, I split myself off from the Continental shelf in a way that I am only now beginning to notice and stitch back together. 1968, the year of political formation for much of my European generation, was for me an American experience, protest and peace rather than revolution and class struggle forming the agenda of our collective imagery. Part of the early 70s were spent in New York City and Cambridge, Massachusetts, as a research student working on American avant-garde theatre. For the next fifteen years I was married to an American (my children still travel on American passports) and Cape Cod was my summer playground. It wasn't till 1982, a gap of almost twenty formative years, that I next visited the European mainland, appropriately enough to give a seminar in Munich on Scottish cinema. During the 80s I have been to France

32

twice, and once, almost by accident, I crossed the Pyrennees into Spain. Finally, last year, I did the proper thing and lazed around for a week on a Greek island.

I am saying all this to establish the tone for this paper, which is one of puzzlement: a lingering puzzlement at how (or how much) to become European, a becoming which I recognise as a political desire but which I have great difficulty in mapping on to experience. Continental Europe, in some sense, somewhat perversely, is my cultural 'other', the 'other' whose difference teaches me my identity. Mainland Europe is my New World, my land of discovery. In Munich, in 1982, rushing wide-eyed from one schloss to another, each sporting the remnants of a courtly culture which still determines present federal and city cultural policy, I discovered, as if for the first time (in the sense in which the formalists talk of the estrangement effect), what it was that Scotland had lost in 1603 when the Scottish crown moved south taking with it any possibility of a continuity of courtly culture and patronage; or what we had lost in 1707 when the Scottish parliament moved south taking with it the benefits and the administrative rationality of the Scottish Enlightenment.

America, on the other hand, for me as for much of my culturally eclectic Scottish generation, is confused with identity, its culture blurs the specificity of my own. There is after all in Glasgow, on Paisley Road West, a Grand Ol' Opry, and Country and Western is the music of choice in Shetland and the Outer Hebrides. At a deeper level, accustomed by American experience to a more or less common language, I have never learned to be completely comfortable as a European, and as a somewhat uneasy tourist, with the process of objectification of the 'other' as 'native' which follows from my inability to speak his or her language.

The one other detail I would add to complete this snapshot of a willing but uneasy European is that my formative cinematic education came in the 70s, in that post-1968 excitement around theory and ideological critique in both film studies and cultural studies. Much of the intellectual energy of that period went into an engagement with Hollywood which would, in the same contradictory moment, criticise it ideologically and legitimise it academically. The engagement with Europe, on the other hand, was highly selective. The films of Godard and Straub-Huillet provided the stick with which to beat bourgeois realism, and the films of Duras and Chantal Akerman began to open up the question of a feminine discourse in cinema. The rest was silence: classified as a European 'art cinema' in which the word 'art' couldn't be spoken without an involuntary curl of the lips. The engagement was with popular culture and political culture. It is only now, with writing about French cinema or German cinema or East European cinema by, for example, Susan Hayward, Ginette Vincendeau and Thomas Elsaesser,[1] that many of us from that generation of film academics are beginning to erode those prejudices and see European cinema, both as a reality and as a possibility, in more complex ways.

I am trying to trace, then, through my own peculiar history, the difficulty of that new feeling which is in the air of *becoming European*: becoming European, that is, not simply as a buyer and seller in the market, but as if for the first time, in a new sense of alignment and identity. Clearly my experience may not be characteristic, and this detour through the personal and through biography may only establish the suspect nature of my European credentials. But it may, on the other hand, key into a hybridisation of identity which is characteristic at least of contemporary Scottish culture – perhaps much more characteristic of a culture which has been trained by history to place itself on the margins than of a metropolitan culture which still believes itself to be at the core.

My point, at any rate, is that even within Britain, at either an individual, a local or a national level (and these are linked by complex histories and geographies) there is no unified way of becoming European and probably no single practical route by which to enter Europe. At the same time, I would be unhappy to follow the route marked out by Jean-Luc Godard towards the isolation of individual consciousness in which there are no identities beyond the personal. There are, in the notion of 'Europeanness', some complex collectivities which it seems necessary to understand.

Clearly the disunity within unification is not peculiar to Britain. In a recent *Marxism Today* there is a piece by Richard Evans on German reunification one year on.[2] As evidence of a lingering disunity he begins the article by citing a number of opinion poll findings: a poll taken in East Berlin in July 1990 showed that only 48 per cent of East Germans felt themselves to be Germans, the rest preferred to think of themselves as 'GDR Germans' or even 'GDR citizens.' 'The poll concluded that it would take at least a decade "to find a new identity in a new Germany".' 'Another striking opinion poll finding', the article continues,

> revealed a surprising degree of ignorance in both parts of Germany about how the other half lived, or indeed even where the other half was. Asked in November 1990 to point out the south-western state of Baden-Württemberg on a map, 71 per cent of easterners proved unable to do so. And 68 per cent of westerners found it impossible to say where the East German province of Thuringia was. ... Easterners thought westerners more arrogant, ruthless, egotistical, mistrustful, self-confident and hostile to children than they were, but

admitted that they themselves were more indecisive, uncertain, lazy and provincial than their western fellow-citizens.[3]

The most dramatic finding, according to the article, was that by January 1991, 86 per cent of easterners felt themselves to be second-class citizens, while only 46 per cent of westerners agreed.

The implied thesis of the article is that this is a serious but temporary glitch on the way to a unified identity. My response to that is that if you turned the map ninety degrees on its axis, and asked the same questions in the north and south of the United Kingdom, you would find that two hundred years after unification the results might look the same. Northerners might feel themselves to be second-class citizens, and southerners would identify that as being symptomatic of the whingeing Scot. Many Scots would probably prefer to identify themselves as Scottish, rather than British, and certainly rather than English. How many southerners could find Cowdenbeath on the map? (How many Glaswegians could?) And it was only recently that I finally discovered exactly where Sheffield was (I was surprised to find it was so far north – it's much more difficult to know where the north of England begins if you live in Scotland). If asked, many Scots and northerners would probably tell you that southerners were more arrogant, ruthless, egotistical, mistrustful, self-confident and hostile to children than they were; though, if pushed, they might admit to being more indecisive, uncertain and provincial – though never lazy. And then, of course, if in turn, you turned that map 180 degrees on its axis and placed it over Italy a hundred years after the Risorgimento, or over France or Spain, you might find the same attitudes going in the opposite direction, with cultural superiorism draining south towards the Mediterranean, and the markers of inferiorism flooding back.

So what do we conclude? We conclude, I think, that becoming European is a process of *endless* becomings and divisions; that it is a process marked by a multitude of histories of uneven development, defined by difference and by quite difficult instability at both the personal and the collective level; and that as soon as it becomes otherwise, as soon, that is, as it is an achieved, reified thing – the European Ship of State – a stable thing which believes in itself, then is the time, precisely, to abandon ship. That kind of identity, national or supranational, which no longer recognises its own differences and instabilities, an identity which is no longer becoming but *has arrived*, full achieved, is a dangerous and almost invariably malign thing.

Homi Bhabha, in his article 'DissemiNation', in *Nation and Narration*,[4] relates this process to what he calls a 'performative time', a time in which the national culture is being performed in a continual present, refusing the ordering discourse of a reifying history or a

35

collective future. Quoting Fanon, he refers to the people's culture as 'the fluctuating movement that the people are *just* giving shape to'.[5] The emphasis he and Fanon put on the '*just*' refers to the liminality of a national culture, to its place on the threshold of enunciation, its shape sensed but never grasped in a single gesture, an identity which always seems about to be but never is, never achieves the stability which can be looked back on. 'The present of the people's history, then,' says Bhabha,

> is a practice that destroys the constant principles of the national culture that attempt to hark back to a 'true' national past, which is often represented in the reified forms of realism and stereotype. Such pedagogical knowledges and continuist national narratives miss the 'zone of occult instability where the people dwell' (Fanon's phrase). It is from this *instability* of cultural signification that the national culture comes to be articulated as a dialectic of various temporalities – modern, colonial, post-colonial, 'native' – that cannot be a knowledge that is stabilised in its enunciation.[6]

By this zone of occult instability I understand Bhabha and Fanon to mean an instability which is concealed behind the aspiration to stability, or behind its illusory identity. In order to represent itself as a national culture instability has to misrecognise itself as stable, collective and representative; but that necessary misrecognition, the political and intellectual will towards identity and unity, is always destabilised by the recognition and the experience of difference and diversity. It seems to me to be that mix of necessary misrecognition, desire for identity, lived experience and difference which characterises the instability of becoming European, or indeed, of becoming Scottish, or English or German.

How does this relate to films like Godard's *Passion*, Denis's *Chocolat*, Almodóvar's *Women on the Verge of a Nervous Breakdown*, Jarman's *The Tempest*?[7] Well, it seems to me to make sense of one characteristic (maybe the only characteristic) which they have in common: a characteristic which may also run through a much wider range of European cinema, and which may help us to think more positively and complexly the opposition 'art cinema'/'popular cinema', or European cinema/Hollywood cinema: a characteristic to which I want to give the provisional and somewhat inadequate, vastly over-general and rather undramatic name – irony.

Irony, which the Concise Oxford Dictionary defines as an 'expression of meaning ... by the use of language of a different or opposite tendency', seems to me to give some consistency of representational form to the knowing misrecognitions and the occult instabilities of

36

identity, individual or collective. In another sense, that of the philosopher Richard Rorty, irony is the belief that there are no sacred words which possess the truth, no final vocabulary which provides guarantees.[8] Or at it widest sense, irony is distance, non-identification with the language one has to use: distanciation, perhaps, but in a wider sense than the formalist prescriptiveness which crept in behind Brecht's theory and practice. In relation to Fanon's and Bhabha's occult instability, to the liminality of identity, irony is the ability to say there is no absolute truth, there is no final vocabulary, there is no real identity, *and yet* ...; where the '*and yet* ...' forms the occulted desire concealed with the ironic distance. This non-identification with a final vocabulary seems to me to characterise in complex ways the films we have been watching. At the risk of essentialism, it seems to me to be a recognisable sensibility (or at least one part of a recognisable sensibility) within modern European traditions in art and culture. When he shrugs at the notion of 'Europeanness', Godard is, ironically enough, playing out precisely the role expected of the European intellectual: secure in his identity as an intellectual he is able to distance himself ironically from any other imaginary collectivity.

In thinking about this, I was reminded of another literary and cultural critic who uses the concept of an occulted sensibility which is both hidden in representations, and determining. In his book, *The Melodramatic Imagination*,[9] a book which has been very influential in academic studies of popular film and television, the American literary critic, Peter Brooks, refers to what he calls the 'moral occult':

If we consider the prevalence of hidden relationships and masked personages and occult passages in Balzac, we find that they derive from a sense that the novelist's true subject is hidden and masked. The site of his drama, the ontology of his true subject, is not easily established: the narrative must push toward it, the pressure of the prose must uncover it. We might say that the center of interest and the scene of the underlying drama reside within what we would call the 'moral occult', the domain of operative spiritual values which is both *indicated within and masked by* the surface of reality. The moral occult is not a metaphysical system; it is rather the repository of the fragmentary and desacralized remnants of sacred myth. It bears comparison to unconscious mind, for it is a sphere where our most basic desires and interdictions lie, a realm which in quotidian existence may appear closed off from us, but which we must accede to since it is the realm of meaning and value. The melodramatic mode in large measure exists to locate and articulate the moral occult.[10]

37

For Brooks, the moral occult lies at the heart of melodrama as a genre, but also at the heart of a melodramatic mode of thought, a melodramatic imagination which Brooks sees as a 'central fact of the modern sensibility'.[11]

The homology between these two occult zones – the moral occult of Brooks and the occult instability of Fanon and Bhabha – seems to me irresistible. For the one, for sensibility underpinned by the moral occult, daily life, discourse, enunciation, representation is desacralised, but is somewhere guaranteed by a residual faith in a sacred word which will unlock the hidden truth: a hidden truth, which can, with effort and through the pressure of language, be discovered behind the surface of representation and enunciation, impregnating them with full meaning. For the other, for the sensibility underpinned by occult instability, enunciation, discourse, representation have to proceed *as if* there were stabilities and identities from which to proceed, but have behind them, as their occult zone, the fact of instability, contingency and irreducible difference. The gap which is opened up between the '*as if*' of identity and the fact of difference seems to me to be the gap represented by the ironic mode. Against Brooks's central fact of the modern sensibility, the 'melodramatic imagination', I therefore want to postulate another central fact, an 'ironic imagination', *the two existing in a complex and dialectical simultaneity.* This is to say, I do not want to postulate a historical progression: 'once we were melodramatic, now we are ironic'; nor a cultural hierarchy: 'high culture is ironic, popular culture is melodramatic'; nor a geographical mapping: 'Europe is ironic, America is melodramatic' (though that one is seductive). All I want to postulate is a dialectic of representational forms, sensibilities and imaginations which resonates with Homi Bhabha's 'dia-lectic of various temporalities – modern, colonial, post-colonial, "native"'.

This is work in progress. Clearly I have more work to do if I am to make this stick, and I am conscious of the particularities, articulations and reconfigurations which lie behind my generalities, and of the slipperiness of a term like 'sensibility'. Here, though, I simply want to point to two currently fashionable temptations in conceiving of an ironic imagination in order that I can distance myself from them.

There is, of course, a familiar, soft-focus, nostalgic irony which refreshes its object without transgressing it. This wisftul irony, as Cairns Craig suggests in a recent *Sight and Sound*, is quickly becoming part of the generic iconography of English mainstream cinema.[12] Craig writes about a whole genre of English films (specifically the Merchant/Ivory adaptations of Forster, but extending much more widely) which is marked by a peculiar relationship to the past, a past which is isolated from the stream of history, focusing on a generation around the First World War which does not know its own past or future. The irony is, of course, that we do; but this is a comfortable and reassuring irony, a sense that we possess but they do not that something has been or is about to be lost: irony rendered as sentimental tragedy. The point I want to make here is that there are no political guarantees built into irony such as were sought, for instance, in discussions of Brechtian distanciation and the progressive text. Having established irony as a sensibility, or as an imaginative mode, there is then a great deal of discrimination to be done within it.

The other pitfall of irony that I want to draw attention to is 'indifference', the indifference of what Peter Sloterdijk calls 'enlightened false consciousness'.[13] Here I simply want to quote Suzanne Moore's *Guardian* review of *Twin Peaks* (and I have to say I quote it as a reluctant addict of *Twin Peaks*.)

I can get off on post-modernism along with the best of the boys but I don't know if I want to any more because the bottom line is that post-modern irony means never having to say you're sorry. Or that you are serious. To complain or even to raise questions about Lynch's treatment of women means you have been caught in the Lynch mob's favourite noose. 'Oh God, you didn't take it seriously, did you? How frightfully unhip to think a scene about torturing women is really *about* torturing women.'

Ambivalence without consequence, the delights of dilemma, and a luxurious quandary become fashion accessories of the post-modern consciousness. What I want to argue is that it is precisely the dialectic, as a still troubling kind of friction, between what I am calling a melodramatic imagination and an ironic imagination, that provides sticking points against, on the one hand, indifference, accommodation and cynical reason, and, on the other hand, against absolute moralities, final vocabularies, and sentimental nostalgias. What Brooks calls the moral occult, although I am uncomfortable with the term, seems to point to a zone in which something serious lurks, a final vocabulary *for me*, something which I cannot or would not enunciate with the confidence of theoretical or political consistency, but which *makes a difference*, or, simply, makes difference. If Fredric Jameson is right that post-modernism is like surrealism without the unconscious, this may be something like the unconscious.[14] To tie it back to questions of nationality and identity and culture, let me return one more time to Homi Bhabha:

Cultural difference must not be understood as the free play of polarities in the homogeneous empty time of the national community. It addresses the jarring of meanings and values generated between the variety and diversity associated with cultural plenitude; it represents the process of cultural interpretation formed in the perplexity of living, in the disjunctive, liminal space of national society.[15]

I am suggesting, then, that European cinema might be conceived as a particular set of dispositions of the ironic and the melodramatic, neither one thing nor the other exclusively, but appearing in changing configurations, sometimes softly reassuring, often indifferent, but always potentially unsettling to the received stabilities.

Within this framework, let me make some brief, but more specific remarks about *Passion*, *Chocolat*, *The Tempest*, and *Women on the Verge of a Nervous Breakdown*, focusing particularly on *Passion*.

The first thing to remark in general terms is the astonishing transformation which has been worked on Godard's film by history. Seeing it for the first time for eight or nine years, I am taken aback by its complex representation of Europeanness, a preoccupation which must always have been there, but was never so apparent. It was, of course, clear in the acknowledgement of the birth of Solidarity, and in Godard's familiar fascination with languages and dialects, but these issues were before the background to what seemed the 'real' engagement with class and sexuality, work and love. Now those European questions – in what language do we speak? what is our relation to the history of European art? where is home? – leap to the front of the screen.

In terms of the dialectic which I am trying to work out, what I want to point to in *Passion* is a new kind of attention to aesthetic beauty. Again, this attention was always there allusively in his early reference to paintings, and particularly in his use of music, and it is quite powerfully there in *One or Two Things I Know about Her*. But in *Slow Motion*, and most particularly in *Passion*, it seems to me to move from the edge of the frame to the centre, *jarring*, in Bhabha's sense, the narrative order – or, more exactly, arresting, with its serenity, the narrative disorder. The farcical, dangerous disorder of the story, the relationships, the language, the instability of identity, the uncertainty of where anyone belongs (and to whom) all exist in a dialectical relationship to the absolute serenity of the tableaux; and it seems to me to be like the kind of dialectic that I am trying to describe. If we take Baudelaire's definition of modernity as 'the ephemeral, the fugitive, the contingent, the half of art whose other half is the eternal and the immutable',[16] the tableaux of *Passion*, drawn from the premodern history of European art, attempt impossibly to flesh out the eternal and the immutable (representing the unrepresentable in rep-

40

resentation itself, in Lyotard's well-worn phrase). They provide the '*and yet* ...' for the instability of everything else, arresting the other narrative (ephemeral, fugitive and contingent) with the possibility of a final meaning, with the liminality which Bhabha refers to, the threshold of a final vocabulary which can never be finally achieved. At the same time they ironically dismantle and erase such a possibility and such a vocabulary. Personified (or objectified) in the body of a woman who can neither hear nor speak, the tableaux are themselves part of an absurd, meaningless and ironic scenario which can never be completed. Nevertheless, the desire to incorporate these sublime images from a European tradition of beauty into an impossible narrative of European cultural identity is the sticking point which stops ironic distance sliding off into the riotous, but ultimately indifferent, farce of *Women on the Verge of a Nervous Breakdown*.

Something similar seems to me to happen in Derek Jarman's degraded, but very beautiful, imagery. In *The Tempest* there is a kind of transgressive veneration for the original text which opens up an ironic gap between the monuments of the national culture and the colonialism on which they are built; but the decadent beauty of the image, the degraded 8 mm, and the fascination of the imagery, prevents that sliding off into comfortable reductiveness.

With *Chocolat*, I found myself, somewhat inevitably, comparing it (considerably in its favour) with *Out of Africa*, where landscape and narrative meld into an organic miasma of sentiment and nostalgia, or with the familiar representations of England's fading glory. In Claire Denis's film the ironic distance is provided by a very precise point of view: both the historical point of view of a complex present in which black America is more disoriented in Africa than the white settler, and the restricted narrative point of view of the child who has not yet learned to naturalise the unspoken orderings of racial and cultural difference – a kind of post-colonial *What Maisie Knew*. But the ironic distance is again anchored against the drift in Bhabha's 'homogeneous empty time' by the proximate intimacy of the land and the landscape.

Each of these, then, seems to me to involve a friction between two kinds of imagination: an ironic imagination, which believes in no final vocabulary, and a melodramatic imagination which says, '*and yet* ...'. Such a friction might best be expressed in oxymorons: 'serious playfulness', 'intimate distance', or Laura Mulvey's phrase, 'passionate detachment'. The films seek to represent difference in ways in which meanings and values jar, and in which difference does not slide off into a mere plurality of identities or an identity of pluralities. It is the possibility of friction and distance, of cultural and multicultural jarring, which might make sense of the desire for a 'Europeanness' in

41

cinema, a desire which is usually lost within the bland, indifferent discourse of European cultural bureaucracy.

At the risk of opening up precisely that discourse of cultural bureaucracy, let me finish by shifting the terms from forms of representation to forms of representativeness. The insistence on a recognition of the instability of cultural identities and on irreducible difference raises questions of practice as well as of form. One way to stabilise what can be represented is to stabilise who can represent it. A real diversity of product, of representations, of identities and discourses has as its precondition a real diversity of modes and sites of production and of points of entry. Here I have a pessimistic scenario and a slightly more optimistic one.

To begin with the optimistic scenario so that I don't devalue my pessimism with cheerfulness, it seems to me that one of the positive effects of the alienating discourse of Thatcherism has been to achieve in some measure exactly the break-up of Britain which Tom Nairn anticipated in the 70s. The voice which came from the centre throughout the 80s was a voice of exclusion, a discourse which could not be recognised as national, and the south-east began to take on the characteristics of a separate island. Alongside post-colonialism, we can begin to think post-metropolitanism, both operating in powerfully decentring ways. This has effects on the way the intellectual agenda is set, and it also has practical effects on production. European initiatives around the various MEDIA projects begin to open up a space in which peripheries begin to speak to each other without passing through the core. Production on the margins begins no longer to be defined by the practices and requirements of the centre. Production deals and consortium arrangements begin to be worked out between producers in small countries. Scottish Television and S4C make arrangements for the exchange of Gaelic and Welsh programming – without asking London.

Of course, the central metropolis still has an undoubted residual hegemony, but what we can begin to detect, in good and bad ways and in varying mixtures of hype and hopefulness, is the development within a service economy of cultural city states. The north–south centralisation begins to erode (at the same time as the country–city centralisation intensifies). We can begin to see cultural change within Britain as no longer a homogeneous thing defined by the experience of the centre, just as we can also begin to see multiculturalism as a force which happens in different forms in different localities rather than as a fixed, essentialised opposition of 'identity' and 'other'. This invites a wildly optimistic scenario in which difference of locality and culture can be represented, almost for the first time, representatively; the map of representations is redrawn to a European and a global scale, a tracing of networks rather than a demarcation of boundaries; and the word 'provincial' disappears or changes its meaning.

But if the optimistic scenario of a post-colonial, post-centre/periphery model of Europe is built on a simultaneous localisation and dissemination of cultural difference, the pessimistic scenario is about how you can begin to think, in any practical way, about the representation of cultural difference in a post-colonial Europe, or a post-colonial Britain, in a context in which black workshops, and indeed regional workshops, cannot be adequately funded, or in which independent feminist film distribution in Britain has all but disappeared.

Notes

1. See, for example, Susan Hayward and Ginette Vencendeau (eds), *French Film: Texts and Contexts* (London: Routledge, 1990); and Thomas Elsaesser, *New German Cinema: A History* (London: BFI Publishing, 1989).
2. Richard Evans, 'Germany's morning after', *Marxism Today*, June 1991, pp. 20–3.
3. Ibid., p. 20.
4. Homi Bhabha, 'DissemiNation', in Bhabha (ed.), *Nation and Narration* (London: Routledge, 1990), pp. 291–322.
5. Ibid., p. 302. The quotations from Fanon in the article come from *The Wretched of the Earth* (Harmondsworth: Penguin, 1969), pp. 174–90.
6. Bhabha, p. 303.
7. This article was written before I had seen *The Time of the Gypsies* or *Young Soul Rebels*. For the record, I think I would extend my basic thesis to *The Time of the Gypsies*, whose so-called 'magic realism' brings together precisely the contradictory qualities of irrational belief and scepticism which are central to the imagination I try to describe. I would have more difficulty with *Young Soul Rebels* – which allows me to say that I am not trying to construct a spuriously universal theory.
8. See particularly, Rorty, *Contingency, Irony and Solidarity* (Cambridge: Cambridge University Press, 1989), p. xv: 'I use "ironist" to name the sort of person who faces up to the contingency of his or her own most central beliefs and desires – someone sufficiently historicist and nominalist to have abandoned the idea that those central beliefs and desires refer back to something beyond the reach of time and chance.'
9. Peter Brooks, *The Melodramatic Imagination: Balzac, Henry James, Melodrama and the Mode of Excess* (New Haven and London: Yale University Press, 1976).
10. Ibid., p. 5
11. Ibid., p. 21
12. Cairns Craig, 'Rooms without a View', *Sight and Sound*, June 1991, pp. 10–13.
13. Peter Sloterdijk, *Critique of Cynical Reason* (Minneapolis: University of Minnesota Press, 1987).

14. Fredric Jameson, *Postmodernism, or, The Cultural Logic of Late Capitalism* (London: Verso, 1991); particularly chapter 3, 'Video: surrealism without the unconscious'.
15. Bhabha, p. 312.
16. Charles Baudelaire, 'The Painter of Modern Life', in *The Painter of Modern Life and Other Essays*, translated and edited by Jonathan Mayne (New York: Da Capo Press, 1986).

EUROPEAN CINEMA ON THE VERGE OF A NERVOUS BREAKDOWN

Stuart Hall

'Screening Europe': but which 'Europe' is this, and what sort of moment is this, for Europe and for European cinema? Despite the triumphalism which is coursing through the capitals of western Europe in anticipation of things to come in 1992, 'Europe' remains an ambiguous and contested signifier. As Philip Dodd asked at the beginning of the discussion, Are we at a funeral or a birth? Are we talking about the death of an old kind of Europe or the birth of a new one? Has Minerva's Owl taken wing, or settled in for another long hibernation? If we look at how Europe is figured in the 'mirror' of the films which provide a context for this discussion, do we see an old identity on the wane or is Europe on the threshold of new ways of representing itself? My overwhelming impression, based on the films we have been looking at, is that, in the very moment of its coming together, Europe reappears as an enigma, an enigma not only to those of us who know Europe well (who are 'in' but not 'of' it, as Paul Gilroy has put it) but also to itself.

This is a critical moment at which to pose the question of how Europe is to be represented. Western Europe is now rapidly propelling itself towards integration, towards some form of political and monetary union and all that follows from the recognition of a 'common homeland'. Eastern Europe's only hope of not reverting to a pre-1941 past seems to be to join in. In the wake of growing global interdependence and the internationalisation of capital and culture, integration is the name of the game. Is Europe, once the centre of the universe, on the verge of reconstituting itself as a kind of regional subculture? In the wake of the disintegration of the old Communist empire and the dissolution of the cold war, many of Europe's internal boundaries are beginning to crumble. Does the dawn of 1992, its *annus mirabilis*, signal the birth of a 'Europe without frontiers'? Can we find these benign tendencies tentatively figured in the mirror of European cinema?

Not very clearly, if we are to trust our reading of these films by

45

Godard, Claire Denis, Jarman and Almodóvar. These are very different films, working within very different cinematic registers and engaging with 'Europe' in very different ways. Nevertheless, what comes across is an overwhelming sense of dislocation before some of these questions – the mark of a disabling irresolution, of blockage, even at times of a kind of hysterical stasis.

Take the collapse of boundaries. Landscape, imagined or real, has always been one of the principal contours, the 'imaginary geography' in Edward Said's phrase, through which identity is figured. It is not only in this century that Europeans have been unsure about where Europe begins and ends. For centuries, what was still known in Columbus's time as 'the green sea of darkness' kept Europe bounded on the west. But on the other side, it had no natural boundary. It used to be the Urals and the Caucasus but, as Eric Hobsbawm has reminded us, in recent years it was withdrawn to the Elbe. Now, once again, it just keeps rolling on.

The problem is, the further east Europe goes, the more it threatens to mutate into something else. There is nothing to be said, in this day and age, for being nostalgic about the cold war, but the cold war did at least give Europe a kind of arbitrary stop. The Berlin Wall, monstrosity that it was, did set up a kind of barrier, real and symbolic. Its awesome brick visage carried a message: 'Beyond this frontier is another kind of Europe, another system, another world.' In a way this reinforced certain old European preconceptions, for the 'real' Europe has always imagined over there as elsewhere, other, the beyond: the frozen wastes, wolves roaming the icy slopes, the mysterious east, barbarians clamouring at the gate of civilisation. With the collapse of the Communist empire and the promise of an alternative social system, the crumbling of the east–west frontier seems, not the opening of another set of rooms in 'our common European home', as Gorbachev hoped, but the opening up of the centre of Europe to new cold winds sweeping down from the steppes. Nationalism, ethnic absolutism, religious bigotry and economic backwardness threaten to descend. As the Ladas and Skodas chug westwards, and the pornography and hamburgers wing their way eastwards, western Europeans are beginning to talk about Russians, Poles, Bulgarians, Hungarians, Romanians and Albanians in the same language they used to reserve for North Africans, Arabs and Turks. No sooner have the barriers collapsed but Europe is busy constructing a new set of margins for itself.

At the same moment as the east–west barrier, which seemed to give 'true Europeans' a sense of who they were, begins to fray and disintegrate, the north–south meridian begins to advance on Europe from the other side. 1992 is a reminder of another, less benign, aspect of Europe – its external face, its outward mission, its missionising force.

It is, after all, the quatercentenary of Columbus's mistake, of Europe's great adventure into 'the unknown' (those millions who lived in 'the unknown', needless to say, already knew it well) and the encounter with other worlds. This will be a celebration calculated to put even Brussels and Strasbourg in the shade: where triumphalism is concerned, we haven't seen anything yet. However, this 'European 1992' is likely to be, at best, an ambiguous, Janus-faced occasion too. For, in the era of globalisation and migration, Europe's 'other' has finally come home to roost. This is also an old European story – expelling the Moors at the front gate only find them creeping in through the back.

Paris, Rome, London, Barcelona, Naples, Frankfurt, like Miami, Los Angeles and New York, are, as someone remarks in Tom Wolfe's *Bonfire of the Vanities*, Third World or 'global' cities. The one-way ticket and the charter flight have brought Europe (which for so long dealt with its colonial outposts at arm's length) within reach of its 'others'. In the age of global production and capital flows and liberalised markets and information systems that exchange messages of their own accord, we are all 'economic migrants' now. The barbarians are already within the gate.

So, who are 'the Europeans' now? How can Europe represent itself? What forms of identity are available to Europe at the end of the twentieth century? How is Europe, with its new and old margins, figured in its own cinema? These ambiguities continue to trouble the question of 'Europe' itself and the ways in which European filmmakers represent it to themselves and others: the problem that Europe now represents for us all. The question of whether Europe is coming or going, how it deals with difference, and whether these films suggest the possibility of new modes of representation or only take us to the edge of an unbridgeable or untranslatable frontier, is the question which these films seem to pose.

We might start with the dissolution of boundaries. These are certainly 'travelling films'. They open with travelling shots, and end in airports. The people in them are constantly moving from one place to another. The finance that makes their travelling possible comes from a hundred different centres. We are in the world of movement, of migration, of dissolving national boundaries, of borderlines. *Women on the Verge of a Nervous Breakdown*, the film most solidly located in its own space, its own city, is of course 'on the verge' of something else, a sort of hilarious insanity. But, as we are reminded at the beginning of Almodóvar's film, Spain has always been at the edge of Europe, represented as archaic, frozen in ancient imperial glories. Actually, some parts of Spain, in the flush of that kind of European inflation that common markets induce and that brings a sudden flush to the cheeks, are extremely modern. It is, at any event, a nice irony that *Women on*

47

the Verge is also the most modern-looking, the most chic-European, of these films. In Europe, we are accustomed to think of national cultures, national histories and national cinemas, but these films are no longer bound within the framework of a national cultural discourse and national forms of representation.

In Godard's *Passion*, the periphery (Poland) has come to town (Paris), too. Jerzy, a Polish film-maker, is in Paris to make a film, which reproduces in film the traditions of European art from which his own country has for so long been excluded. This high, civilising motive is constantly set off against and undercut by the messy, squalid business of film-making. The actual business of cultural production subverts culture. Godard, the European film-maker, uses the cinema to deconstruct the illusion of European art. The project is literally impossible, so it is no surprise that Jerzy's film keeps starting and stopping, and doesn't seem to get made. European art refuses to remain in that serene repose we associate with culture and the contemplative life. The tableaux vivants keep returning to life, the still lives move. That inner light that floods the Rembrandts is the lighting on the set that works for nobody. 'I need a story': but there isn't one. Everyone wants one, but no one can quite tell it.

In the older forms of cinematic alienation, people were locked into their own isolation, into silence. The people in *Passion* sort of understand one another. The Poles and other illegal immigrants speak a kind of French. Many of the French speak Parisian French like a kind of Polish. We are in the world of dialects, of *argots*, of polyglot hybridity. In a sense, everyone is now 'in translation'. On the other hand, no one understands quite enough. 'I am not certain what it is you are saying,' 'I don't understand the way you talk,' 'I don't understand very well,' they say. *Passion* is also a film of, and about, missed understandings. Godard's script is, in the usual way, seriously dislocated linguistically. Image and sound are constantly out of sync. At one level, this has always been Godard's way of interrogating his own cinematic discourse, undermining its naturalistic claims. In *Passion*, the strategy of interruption is what permits him to put language itself, in the context of the new hybridised Europe, under partial erasure. Indeed, *Passion* uses the cinema and film-making itself as metaphors of dislocation.

Passion seems to work through a cycle of displacements. Art/cinema, the central metaphor, sets off a series of them, along a metonymic chain of equivalences: art/cinema, cinema/work, work/pleasure, pleasure/power. The signifiers slip with little hope of stabilisation 'Work is pleasure at different speeds,' one character says. 'I'm working,' she adds – on film: 'I'm working at loving.'

If anything can be said to represent or stand for Europe, it is, on the one hand, the great European ideas (progress, enlightenment, reason, democracy) and, on the other hand, European art and culture. *Passion* moves continuously between the aesthetic forms of European painting and the frenzy of film-making. The dismantling of this central metaphor gives Godard's movie its transgressive quality. Nevertheless, the effect is unsettling. When the 'still lives' begin to move, they unleash disorder, a kind of naked violence. The objects of this violence are the women. Many of them illegal immigrants from Europe's margins, surviving precariously in the informal economy, the women are harrassed both as the outworkers in the sweatshop and as 'extras' in the film, cheated and chased by both the director and the *patron*. (Godard seems to retain some sneaking sympathy for the director, no doubt out of sympathetic identification – the money to finance the film is always being promised and failing to materialise – but he seems to me to be a first-class slob.) When the police stop chasing the women through the factory, the knights on horseback in the tableaux unfreeze and start their pillaging and marauding. The women protest but seem trapped and vulnerable in the marginalised spaces where love, sex, work and film-making circulate. It is hard to know what to do, or what Godard intends to do, with these images of patriarchal violence. They are not contained by any dramatic staging or ironic distance. They are literally on the loose.

When Europe attempts to encounter itself at its edge, so to speak, as it does in Claire Denis's *Chocolat*, is there any more controlled, less hysterical, less internally dislocated way of its confronting or coming to terms with the past? Paradoxically, *Chocolat* is the only real attempt at a post-colonial text among these films. You might think *The Tempest* ought to occupy this space, but Jarman's *Tempest* is (deliberately, one must suppose) not a 'post-colonial' text at all. *Chocolat*, however, *is* an attempt to say something about Europe from its margins. There are some simple sentimentalities at work here, and even a touch of the exotic. But the core of the film, what I would call the 'colonial family romance', is established with great insight and sensitivity. The 'colonial family romance' consists of the father (the European administrator), the madame, the child and the servant. This quadrilateral of power, sexual and other relations is the discursive field across which *Chocolat* mainly operates. The intricate reversals – of love, authority, dependency – between the child and Protée the African servant are a beautifully judged commentary on the way power and desire, authority and intimacy are doubly inscribed in the colonial relationship. Only so long as the child, France, remains a child is the 'romance' between her and the servant (the two 'sibling' dependants) tenuously permissible, and it can't last. The effort of the grown-up France to rediscover this 'lost' colonial world is doomed to failure. As Freud observed, 'He [she] is turning away from the father whom he [she] knows today to the 'father' in whom he [she] believed in the earliest years of his [her] childhood; and his [her] phantasy is no more than the expression of a regret that those happy days have gone.'

Chocolat also contains one sweet symbolic moment of colonial revenge (films like this often contain moments which incite a sort of surplus pleasure which eludes the control of the filmic discourse). When I was a teenager, in Kingston, we used to go every Saturday afternoon to the matinee showing at the Carib Cinema, and one memorable feature of these visits were those illicit moments of pleasure which had everything to do with the audience and precious little to do with the movie. One such occasion was when Rita Hayworth slaps the hero in *Gilda* and, without a pause, he slaps her right back. This exercise of patriarchal discipline had the male members of the audience, I recall, standing and shouting for more. There is a moment like that for me in *Chocolat*, when Protée throws the white hippie, Luke, and his back-pack off the verandah. A film which is able to say to those European hippies who think it's fun to 'make out' in Africa for a white man, 'Why don't you go home?' has a lot going for it. This ambivalent European figure, who quotes from European high literature while seducing the madame, on the one hand, and insists on using the 'boy's' (that is, men servant's) shower, on the other, deserves what he got: his come-uppance.

I'm not sure the madame quite deserved what she got. Nevertheless, the moment when she waits for Protée in the dark on her knees behind the curtain, overcome by the sensuous beauty of his body, and he, silently refusing what she offers, instead makes her stand up, is a remarkable moment for the European cinema. But what is powerful about *Chocolat* is not what happens but what doesn't. It is a film of refusals, of barred intimacies, of turnings away, of meetings that don't come off, of relationships in the past that cannot be recovered, of a colonial world that is gone for ever. The aptly-named France, who has returned to reconnect with her past, discovers its impossibility. The black American cannot 'find himself' in Africa either. 'Here, I'm nothing. A fantasy.' 'Run away quick,' he advises France, 'before you get eaten up.' The faint possibility of something between them, the two outsiders, is unrealised. She tentatively proposes. He gently refuses. When she finally decides not to go on but to go back to France, Protée – a modern Protée, no longer the 'houseboy', but just another airport baggage-handler – can be seen in the distance, talking and laughing with his mates, oblivious of her and us. But she doesn't see him and he doesn't see her. They are both in the travelling business, but in different time frames. Their trajectories cross, but do not meet.

Chocolat is about the dislocations produced by Claire Denis's disciplined refusals, the refusal of absolution. There may come a time when France and Africa can meet again, on different terms, but for now it is either too early or too late for such easy narrative conclusions. And the one thing which Africa should not, at this moment, be required to do is to forgive Europe anything.

Chocolat is a post-colonial text, as it were, by default. Recently, there has been some criticism of the spate of films coming out of or about Africa made by white film-makers which have the European rather than the African experience at their centre. *Chocolat* suggests that this may be the only kind of film European film-makers should be making about Africa just now. It may be time for Europeans to confront what colonisation has done to *them* rather than instantly taking on the white man's burden, once again, of speaking for the 'other'.

The Tempest, on the other hand, has been reread as the classic 'post-colonial' text. But this is the one reading which Derek Jarman steadfastly refuses. 'Otherness' is figured here in almost every other register, apart from race. Paradoxically, Jarman has produced a transgressive but essentially white *Tempest*. Of course, there is nothing actually in the text of *The Tempest* which requires us to think of the New World, and anyway film-makers are at liberty to place it where they want (*Prospero's Books* takes place mainly in the wonderfully spacious and well-peopled chambers of the inside of Peter Greenaway's head). In *Colonial Encounters* Peter Hulme makes an excellent case for locating the text of *The Tempest* in a dual topography. The play, he argues, sets the discourse of the 'Mediterranean' and the discourse of the 'Bahamas' against and within one another, and these are 'the linguistic and narrative force fields [which] we bring to the play to disclose its meanings'. At this historic moment Jarman's refusal of this double repertoire is, to say the least, puzzling. The puzzle persists, despite the wonderfully imaginative *mise en scène*: the extraordinary moment of the sailor's hornpipe; Sycorax's hovel; the lurching and weaving advance of Caliban and the plotters up the stairs; the coming of light (in a film shot in almost permanent semi-darkness and gloom) as the masque unfolds – 'expectancy crowned by sudden revelation'. The 'Stormy Weather' sequence is a moment of sheer Jarmanesque genius, the incongruous transformed into sheer magic.

There is a wonderful performance by Caliban, embodiment of all the standard images of the sexual (and other forms of) the perverse. And yet, in the end, I am not sure that, in these two films about Europe and 'otherness', *Chocolat* and *The Tempest*, there isn't a kind of transgressive quality in the very humanised and to some extent sentimentalised Protée that is absent in Caliban. This impression may be reinforced by the fact that the most profound refiguring of the inversions of relations of power in Jarman's *The Tempest* are to be found, not where we would expect, in Caliban, but in the unsung 'hero' of this film, Ariel. Here is a wonderful study of the 'subaltern', around which so much recent post-colonial criticism has circled, captured in that startling image of Ariel, waiting, waiting, waiting to be released; of Ariel behind glass, in his overdetermined subservience.

The least post-colonial in its reference, the least obviously European in its references, the least confident about the certainties of its 'grand narrative' status, is Almodóvar's *Women on the verge of a Nervous Breakdown*. This is a film which, by working scrupulously within its limits, most effectively breaks boundaries. Here at last is 'modern Europe', chickens in the penthouse and all. The taxi is a veritable cathedral of consumption on wheels. Every necessity of modern life is available in the back seat: eyedrops, tissues, cigarettes that you can't smoke, fifteen magazines in a variety of European languages ... Forget magical realism. This is the 'magical absurd' – Europe, from the bottom up, in its genuinely hybridised form.

The secret of Almodóvar's film seems to lie in its profound adaptation of a sort of 'wild' soap-opera narrative structure: confessions to the police, barbiturates in the *gazpacho*, everything in the fridge. What is most transgressive about *Women on the Verge* is precisely its bottom-up, ground-level, low-life cunning. From this vantage point, it is literally impossible to see Europe as male and magisterial. Everything has been transposed into the 'feminine' register. What men would see as the usual feminine disorder is simply what life is like. The insane logic which drives the plot is, from this point of view, a perfectly normal state of affairs. Men, on the whole, drive women crazy and women spend most of their lives on the verge of a nervous breakdown. After all, as one of her friends complains to Pepa, 'Look at what the Arab world has done to my life!'

What is curious is that Almodóvar's hilarious set-ups, farcical reversals and camp post-modern pastiches allow him to construct one of the few 'authentic' (*sic*) moments in these films – meaning, by authentic, simply something that pierces the surface of the narrative and takes it to another level. After Pepa's hilarious ride to the airport on the back of the motor bike and her melodramatic rescue of Ivan, she just looks at him and remarks in a matter-of-fact way, 'I saved your life – and that's it.' Moments like that appear to come, not from engaging the grand narratives of love and art and culture and cinema direct, but by sneaking up on them from the side or, as Almodóvar has chosen to do, working straight off the edge of its own hysteria.

What is the dislocation through which all these films, in their different ways, appear to suggest Europe is currently passing? Is it a profound, a productive one, which opens the possibilities of new identities

– not the recovery of an old centre or the replacement of one centre by another, but of the opening of a dialogue between the margins? So far, their most compelling moments seem to be moments of recognition of the deep but as yet impassable barriers before which Europe finds itself.

The only place among the films shown on this occasion where it was possible to glimpse a celebration (albeit an innocent one) of hybridity and difference, and a language of difference which, for all its problems, felt new, was in Isaac Julien's *Young Soul Rebels*. As it happens, this was also the only film we saw which contained the image of pleasure and desire not threatened by instant disaster. This was the affair, culminating in the tender, erotically passionate and convincing love-scene between the black, gay Soul Boy, Caz, and Billibud, the white S.W.P. punk militant. Now *that* could be the start of something new – a new kind of 'European' story.

DISCUSSION

Philip Dodd

We have heard three very rich papers which I have no intention of trying to summarise, although there did seem to me to be a family resemblance: that of the provisionality of the identities into which we need to move. There also seem to be very different views about how these new positions are to be realised. I keep thinking of the phrase that Ien quoted from Godard, which is that you have to live stories before you invent them. I think it may actually be the other way round, that you have to invent stories before you can live them. Stuart's reference to the end of *Young Soul Rebels* I think is a very good example of this need to invent stories before they are actually lived.

Question from audience

Isn't there an ease with which we glibly speak of post-colonialism, as it were, ignoring what was going on in Ethopia and in the Gulf War, for example? Isn't there in reality a new colonialism abroad which is rather brutal?

Ien Ang

I think that's true. I think there are many, many ways in which we can speak about post-colonialism. One of the important tasks at this conference is to speak about what it means for Europe. Much of the discussion and debate about post-colonialism tends to come from outside Europe, and somehow I think it's quite ironic to see how the theme of post-colonialism is now being discussed within Europe. But I also think it's very important to see how that theme is being articulated in a very different way in Europe compared with other parts of the world. For Europe, it's a post-colonialist identity that needs to be forged, as John has said, whereas in other parts of the world, post-colonialism means emergence out of a derivative identity. And, of course, recent developments do complicate the matter, because there are a lot of neo-colonialisms and neo-imperialisms around at the moment, but that's the measure of the uneven process of development that we constantly find ourselves in. What's important now is to think of what this whole set of issues means within Europe, because somehow Europe has often been able to successfully erase itself from this whole problem. That's why it is necessary for Europe to think of its own position.

John Caughie

The significance of the 'post', in terms of post-history, post-Marxism, post-modernism and post-colonialism, is that it now actually marks a turning point: once there was colonialism, now we are somewhere else. I find it very difficult to conceive of a post-colonialism which means that we are no longer in a colonial situation; 'post', rather, is actually about how that colonialism is being renegotiated. And it seems to me that renegotiation is historically determined, that different parts of this island have different experiences of a colonial past, and that even within this island the conceptions of post-colonialism, and the kind of renegotiation it involves, are going to be quite different. And if you spread that across Europe, you find various different kinds of renegotiations going on.

Colin MacCabe

What is interesting was the decision of the German SDP last week to absolutely refuse the use of Nato as an out-of-area force. It seems to me that if you're talking about the current politics, the issue is how far Europe will simply go along with current American imperialism, and it seems to me that a lot of the answers to that will come about in the extent to which one can produce an alternative notion of what Europe is doing politically. So the questions we're addressing today are absolutely part of the key questions relating to the current moment.

55

Comment from audience

Nothing much was said about eastern Europe, and I think in terms of the film industry it's quite important to realise that eastern Europe is very much a part of Europe now. State subsidies which, paradoxically, in the past have enabled eastern European film-makers to make some exceptionally good movies have gone. So the idea of a common European identity simply does not work, in terms of the divisions which are still going to exist in the context of financing film-making. It seems to me that this ought to be talked about in the European Community. Furthermore, the domination of the European Community in Europe, and its implications for cinema, is something which I think we perhaps ought to say something about.

Philip Dodd

The logic of the position, which certainly needs to be attended to in a sense, is, who speaks on behalf of whom? I should like to feed into those comments something from Ien's paper; it's something that I have got inside me in terms of the dangers of 'narrow-minded nationalisms'. Now certainly for central Europe, those things don't seem narrow-minded nationalisms. The struggle now, for instance, of Slovakia to become separate from Czechoslovakia, the fragmentation of Yugoslavia – 'fragmentation' may be a pejorative way of putting it – the reorganisation of Yugoslavia into a number of kind of ethnic nations, the relationship between those nations and the nation-state, these are certainly extremely important. There are moments when this seems to be returning us to 1914, as it were, to that moment of the Austro-Hungarian Empire; and obviously there are anxieties around that. I raise all this because I think it is extremely important to acknowledge that anxieties around 'narrow-minded nationalisms' derive from 'western' Europe rather than central Europe. And yet the 'western' sense of nationalism and central Europe's sense of nationalism is a radically different matter.

Stuart Hall

I think that we have to recognise that the films we have seen are quite partial, inevitably partial because it's a selection; but I think we should recognise the consequences of that selection. One of the things I was trying to say was that, apart from a very particular perspective in *Chocolat*, and a certain way of not finding it in *The Tempest*, there

56

isn't really what I would call a post-colonial text here. And one of the reasons why I quoted the remark in Almodóvar's film, 'Look what the Arab world has done to me,' is because, in the first instance, of its shocking provincialism. On the other hand, I don't go to a Spanish film director to find out how Arabs see the world. That's why I think most of us have centred on the whole question of the dislocation or de-colonisation of Europe. It's the European imaginary, in the face of historical change, that we've been trying to talk about and to figure out. How 'otherness' is experienced – indeed, how Europe is experienced from the periphery – would require another range of films to see. So I think we have to recognise what is the terrain of this conversation and what's left out of it.

Ien Ang

I think it is becoming clear how dangerous it is to invest too much desire into this idea of European identity as a super-national or unifying stable thing. As someone who has lived in Europe for a long time, but at the same time not really finding myself an essential European person, I've looked at developments in eastern Europe with a lot of difficulty. I've been in eastern and central Europe several times, and I do feel when I'm in that part of the world that there are so many differences and so many ignorances on both sides that it's very difficult to find a certain sense of commonality. And I think that's one of the things that we need to recognise, that these differences make a huge impact on how we see each other and how we can find ourselves being part of the same continent.

Comment from audience

One of the things that was very interesting, and more complicated, is that, yes, we ought to be also talking about other nationalisms, other national experiences, but we should also consider certain super-national experiences such as the Muslim experience, the migrant experience and the Gypsy experience.

Vladimir Padunov

I'd like to challenge some things which have been said. If you are going to acknowledge the existence of a 'central Europe' and an 'eastern

Europe' then the problem that I'm hearing is not the problem of defining European identity on the basis of western European identity, but that the problem of the sunset centrism demonstrated here obscures the fact that western Europe is actually the periphery for Europe. It is, in reality, a question of the margins dictating to the centre and to the other margins what the identity of the whole is. And that identity is not shared by central Europe or by eastern Europe, and it has never been shared by the Soviet empire, except in its external appearances. Our clothes are European, and our eyes are Asian. Our minds are European, and our hearts are Asian. In effect, to establish European identity by a sunset centrism is to distort the notion of identities in Europe, it is to marginalise the problem in a way that doesn't immediately become apparent, and it is to distort the whole national and notion of identity in Europe.

John Caughie

Somebody said last night that the problem for Europe is not America, the problem is actually new identities and new communities within Europe. But I think in some sense I've taken that on board. You talk about Europe and the 'other', but I think a much more helpful contribution is that notion of the 'other' Europeans, the Europeans who are not included in the notion of Europeanness. That ties into what Ien was saying about the difference between European identity and identities within Europe. Because it's quite clear to me that the question we're addressing just now is actually how you re-articulate these new identities, how you incorporate them into the image of Europeanness. I don't even think it can actually be done in relation to national boundaries. I think that the city/country divide is extremely powerful as well – there are quite different concepts of belonging between an urban population and a rural population – and that all of these categories are actually being fragmented. In some sense what we're trying to find out is, if you like, a European cinema which can represent all of those fragments of identity. I have this sense that there is actually almost a consensus around this notion of identity, though I haven't in fact heard anybody who's actually stood up and said there is a European identity – even that there is a British identity or there is a national identity. I think, really, where the debate has to go is actually, how do you incorporate the identities which are left in the place of that sort of unifying identity? It's how you actually find some way of expressing collectivity, as it were. The distinction that Godard was making last night between national cinemas and film-makers, in some sense he

58

posed a kind of problem between identity – European identity and national identity – and individuals. I suppose what I'm trying to find a way to think is, how in that gap you then organise collectivities. How do you organise, think about, express, recognise the collectivities in between?

Question from audience

Just to continue the point that was made, the question of whether migration is central to European identity. Someone said recently that Europe didn't have an identity, it had regional identities. And because there was a massive migration between regions in Europe, that was what was creating European identity: European identity was being forged in relation to ethnicity within those regions. So people from Europe moving to other parts of Europe were discovering their own identity. I want to know whether the panel think that that is true and whether this has anything to do with redefining Europe's own Eurocentrism.

Stuart Hall

I do think that migration is part of the new terrain of articulations which the term 'Europe' might refer to. I think it's a very important part of it. It's not easy to make the distinction that governments are always trying to make, between free and forced migration. Most migrations are a little bit of both. One has to look very specifically, I think, at what the actual contours of current migration are, because those migrations very frequently represent in part the search (which I think is certain to be impossible) for some atavistic national or other ethnic identity which can restabilise the kind of fractioned identities of which Europe now consists. Another issue, that of forced migration, is of course the migration from European periphery to European centre. So, if you just say 'migration', you get the notion of, you know, everybody set free, as it were, by cheap air travel. But in fact these are very controlled, very highly structured movements, and at the same moment as they appear to dissolve old boundaries they actually reconstitute new ones. I think we aren't anywhere close to seeing what those new configurations of imaginary migrated spaces in Europe are likely to be. But I'm sure that it is very much at the centre of the story. I think if you saw Europe figured from the periphery, the question of

59

migration would have been absolutely at the centre, the trope of migration would have figured everywhere, because migration is the twenty-first-century story. It's exactly what I was trying to say when I invoked the metaphor of Frankfurt, Naples, Rome, LA, being migrated cities, Third World cities, cities in which the native populations are increasingly the minorities. I think that the patterns of migration are very much the way in which the stories of the periphery are likely to be told and retold; and no doubt there are ways in which Europe itself is beginning to face the disconcerting undermining of its old landscapes as a consequence of migration, leading to exactly that kind of hybridity which people have been talking about. But I don't find that theme very profoundly figured in these films. One of the things that I felt about *Passion* is that, in fact, it does seem to be located in a Europe where the boundaries are dissolving, but it isn't about that issue of the movement of peoples across boundaries, which is going to be a central part, it seems to me, of the wider European story.

Comment from audience

I should like to return to the question of the Gypsies, because I think that one of the problems is not simply the logistical problem of having seen the film or not having seen the film, but rather the fact that the question of colonisation is a false posing of the question when we are dealing with Gypsy culture. I think a more rational approach has to do with the kind of enforced mandatory criminalisation of Gypsy culture, particulary in urban societies, which is a refusal on the part of authorities, from the municipal level all the way up, to engage in any kind of dialogue with Gypsy communities about what their needs are and how those needs might be accommodated within society. This is true whether we're talking about solidarity with the Bulgarian Gypsies or Yugoslav Gypsies, the Russian Gypsies or western European Gypsies, regardless of religious orientation. In that respect it seems to me that the whole issue of colonisation is one that lags behind mandatory criminalisation; that the other nations which come into the European centre experience what Gypsy culture has already experienced for centuries – namely, to be of one's own ethnic identity is already to be perceived as a criminal. The urban Gypsy is in the unfortunate position of being regarded as a criminal because Gypsy society is non-urban. The film *Time of the Gypsies* helps us understand Gypsy culture better than posing the question as colonisation or post-colonial culture.

Comment from audience

It seems to me that a crucial point in this debate is the production and distribution of narratives, because identities are formed through our experiences and through how our experiences are narrativised, how they are told in stories. And it seems to me that western Europe's position on the periphery is indeed a true one, but its own centrism, if you like, has been instructed by the fact that it has a rich enough film and television culture which is able to reflect its own narratives, its own representations, back to itself. Europe has the luxury of being able to defend itself even against America. This is what places us in that Eurocentric position. It obscures, if you like, its position on the periphery.

Comment from audience

I'm having trouble with the use of agency within what people say. I want to know who is going to do the imaging and imagining and the revisioning that we're talking about. I just wanted to link it to two things that were said yesterday. One was Colin MacCabe's point about not wanting to get involved in the cultural bureaucracy of Brussels, which I can understand. The other is to ask something about why, in situations where groups need to articulate identity, this doesn't happen. I think the point I'm trying to make is that the kind of national cinematic formation Godard was talking about was related to organisation and money and state support, and that differently constituted identities can't just pop up from nowhere. It's somebody's job to facilitate this, for the question relates to a variety of things like education systems, funding systems, organisations and culture. Culture doesn't just grow, it actually also gets born.

Stuart Hall

I think that the terrain of *Young Soul Rebels* is not a Caribbean reference. But I think it is located in the tensions and contradictions of the migrated situation, which is not about the experience of migration but rather about the migrated. And there, I think, you have to see the transgressions working differently. It's quite true that both the stereotypes and the moments of opening are sometimes figured in racial terms, sometimes figured in sexual terms. It is that complexity of languages which I like in the film. What I think is transgressive about it is that the film doesn't settle by saying things in the registers that we're accustomed to hearing them: the register that you might expect to be located in race, colour, ethnicity, is sometimes spoken or enunciated in the sexual register. And it's exactly the confusion of that hybridising of registers that I think is exciting about this film. It doesn't always come off, but that doesn't matter. And as for the stereotype of the black body, I simply want to affirm that black men looking at black bodies is a pretty transgressive thing to happen in any cinema, especially in the European cinema just now. To represent that moment as a genuine moment of erotic pleasure, to judge from the films that we've seen, it's not easy to talk about love; it's not easy to talk about sex either, you know. So I experience these things as very powerful, controversial, contestatory, exploratory images. I think if one got into the argument more fully there are a lot of fluctuations in the film – but there are moments which come right out of the filmic structure and absolutely rivet one to a different language. The point that I was trying to make about the other films, bold and wonderfully complex as they are, is that I didn't feel that I saw many such moments. I felt a much greater control of the surface logic and narratives of the films, and I didn't feel that moment when the image kind of broke through a set of frames and actually said something else. So, that's why I would still hold to the importance of that moment in the film, although I think that the question of how one reads the film as a whole is still to come.

John Caughie

Can I just pick that up? I agree absolutely with what Stuart is saying, but I do have difficulties with the representation of Scottish people in *Young Soul Rebels*. I think the reason I make the point is that as well as thinking about making films, that there are different ways of making films, there are obviously, quite clearly, different ways of watching films, and that different things will arrest our attentions within the films. And that in some sense the idea of watching as a European is as difficult as the idea of making as a European, and that we in a sense transform films by our own experience.

THE FILM-MAKERS PANEL
Introduction

Duncan Petrie

This panel of film-makers was invited to reflect the heterogeneity, in terms of ethnicity, gender and sexuality, of contemporary European film-making voices. They were Felix de Rooy from the Netherlands, Isaac Julien (whose first full-length feature *Young Soul Rebels* had received its first public screening the previous evening) and John Akomfrah from Britain, Chantal Akerman from Belgium and Claire Denis (whose film *Chocolat* was one of the contextualising screenings) from France. With the exception of Chantal Akerman, all the panel members could be described as in the early stages of their film-making careers. Like the other participants at the conference, they had viewed the selected films in order to focus on relations between broad concepts of Europe, identity and audiovisual culture. Their varied responses represented here cast new light on questions central to the conference.

Felix De Rooy

As a black European film-maker with Caribbean roots, when I think about the question of European identity there are two elements which immediately strike me: European identity in relation to the Third World, to the colonial past, and European identity in relation to the United States. With regard to the second element, I detect a certain European phobia towards the American cinema which comes out of the perceived threat of American culture. After all, what is the United States but an ex-European colony which has turned into a multicultural, multiracial society. Europe is afraid of this because it feels threatened by exposure to other cultures which might dilute 'authentic' European identity. This is reflected in what I call the Third World aspect of Europe: the fact that Europe is turning into a society like the United States which is no longer monoracial and monocultural. Such processes are viewed as a negative impurification of traditional culture, a fear of loss of identity which amounts to little more than an adorned xenophobia.

Turning to the films screened for this conference, *The Tempest* is interesting for me because in Caliban we have a European image of Third World culture – the cannibal, the servant, the violent, stupid and deceitful being – a classic example of the racism and negative stereotyping against which Europe has, as far back as Shakespeare's time, defined its own identity. *Passion*, on the other hand, demonstrates the desperate need of white European culture to renew itself without opening up to other cultural influences. Despite a wealth of evidence to the contrary, Europe has constantly denied the influence of other cultures and races on the structure of its own identity. But what you are left with is a blind retrospective re-evaluation of familiar images which fails to recognise the historical relationship between Europe and the Third World, the Americas and Africa.

Godard suggested yesterday that world cinema is basically made by white boys, which leads me to consider the relationship between sexism, xenophobia, and homophobia in European society. I find that the attitude of white women film-makers to other cultures, other races, and the emotional interaction between these 'alien forces' and white Europeans, is much more positive and open. *Chocolat* is a good example of this. But it is not only white women who have to respond to the images created by their male counterparts, black Europeans also have to speak out. They must contribute to the transformation of constructions of European cultural identity by reinterpreting both the present and the past. The analysis of our past has very often been through the perspective of the dominant white culture which seeks to deny outside cultural presence and influence in Europe. The re-evaluation of our past is very important for the evaluation of our present.

A film like *Young Soul Rebels* answers the white boys' cinema by demonstrating the relationship between racism and 'macho' heterosexism. Isaac Julien's film brings out the psychological links between macho fears of an alien culture and of homophobia, which are rooted in the repression and denial of something enormously attractive. This is the dilemma of the male who has been conditioned to think in terms of heterosexual norms, and the moment he is confronted by alternatives to these norms he panics and strikes out against them.

There is therefore a strong need for an alternative to the white heterosexual male viewpoint. The kind of cinema represented by films like *Young Soul Rebels* has a unique ability to express the complex reality we all live in. Cinema is the strongest form of popular culture, and popular culture is one of the most important aspects in the shaping of our cultural consciousness (and unconsciousness) in terms of our relations to class, sex, spiritual and cultural conflicts.

Isaac Julien

What I want to do is talk about the construction of 'Europe' as a kind of national identity, and the way in which black subjects are located within that context. In Europe there is a fiction that only white subjects can be called European and the fixing of the category 'other' to black people is successfully achieved through the repetition of stereotyped images and by various forms of policing. For example, in Switzerland, where Jean-Luc Godard lives, Kurdish refugees seeking political asylum have been effectively policed into hiding by the authorities. In addition, second-generation blacks born in Switzerland are having their national identity questioned simply because they are not white. This fixing of non-white people and culture has the effect of rendering 'black movies' as somehow marginal and in doing so denies the complexities of black cultural spaces in Europe. To illustrate by way of a rather crude point: if Picasso had been black, would we have labelled his work as just 'black art'?

Why is it, then, that the complexities of black artistic practices are reduced to this monolithic containment? And why are Kurdish refugees conceived of as a threat to Swiss national identity? Some of these questions, I think, can be answered by way of introducing some concepts around the idea of modernity in contemporary Europe.

Marshall Berman has suggested that to be modern is to find ourselves in a paradoxical environment that promises adventure, power, joy, growth and the transformation of ourselves and the world, while simultaneously threatening to destroy everything we have, everything we know and everything we are. The negative side of this paradox is an articulation of the discourse of white paranoia in relation to the 'other' because the cultural realities of post-colonialism demand a reconceptualisation of national identity.

Stephen Ross also has some very interesting things to say about modernity. He talks about two responses to the experience of modernity. On the one hand, multiplicity, contradiction, flow, a celebration of heterogeneity and difference. On the other, a rigidity, a domination, a totalitarianism represented by a redrawing of the European borders and immigration controls (the idea of Fortress Europe). The latter response has contributed to the rebirth of discourses around nationalism and the new European racism.

What I hope is that black independent cinema can shed light on these debates, to make the modern experience of living in Europe a

65

more pluralistic one for both black and white people, to challenge the construction of black and white identities and to move beyond the question of what is a 'Black cinema' or even a 'European cinema.' In my own work what I have tried to do is to repoliticise the gaze of both black and white spectators. In both *Looking for Langston* and *Young Soul Rebels* I am interested in exploring the way in which the white subject projects his repressed sexuality on to blacks, constructing them in fantasy as the sexual paragon. In *Young Soul Rebels*, this phenomenon is effectively explored through the character of Ken, a white homosexual, whose inability to deal with his own repressed desire for black men leads him to murder the object of that desire. The black response, on the other hand, is to desexualise their own black cultural icons (as in the case of Langston Hughes) and hence sanitise them, at the cost of any ambivalent reading of their work. What so unsettled the Langston Hughes estate in America, which tried to censor the film, was the prioritisation of the scopic – the image replaced the word and showed what could not be said. As Lacan has stated, it is only the image which can transgress the law of the father. Bell Hooks has suggested that *Looking for Langston* reconstructs and reinvents a history of black gay sexuality while simultaneously problematising the notion of secrecy and repression. Images in the film pose the question: what form does desire take in that space where recognition is dangerous and denied?

Denial raises the danger of unambivalent reading and discursive closure, and I think it's interesting that such lines of thought are being reproduced in relation to *Young Soul Rebels*. And obviously, what I want to do in my films is redevelop these debates in a different light, to open up debate and discussion.

Claire Denis

I come to this conference as someone raised in European culture but born outside Europe. I want to begin by referring to a line from *Passion*: 'Il faut vivre les histoires avant les inventer' – you have to live stories before you invent them. This for me is an important statement. I believe that when you make a documentary you concentrate on the 'other', but when you make fiction you talk about yourself. Cinema is therefore a very personal medium, and if European cinema is anything it is a reflection of subjective European experiences.

When I was making *Chocolat* I think that I had a desire to express a certain guilt I felt as a child raised in a colonial world. When the film was completed I was asked to write a piece on it for the press booklet. Unsure of what to write, I found an introduction to an anthology of

Black literature and poetry by Jean-Paul Sartre which suggested that for three thousand years the official view of the world had been a white view and he now welcomed an alternative – the view from those who had been watched, what they saw when they looked at us, the white Europeans. I put this in the booklet because I thought that there was very little else I could say: knowing I was white, I tried to be honest in admitting that *Chocolat* is essentially a white view of the 'other'.

Raising money for the film was difficult because of the subject matter, but significantly, I did not experience any problems in actually discussing colonialism – unlike the censorship experienced by film-makers in France after the Algerian war. I was, however, strongly advised to construct an affair between Protée, the male black servant in the film, and the white woman. The producers saw this outcome as good box office. But this would have totally destroyed what the film was about for me, so I resisted the pressure to alter the script. When it came to doing the scene in which Protée resists the possibility of a sexual encounter with the woman, I shot it quickly in one take, before anyone could even attempt to suggest an alternative. I know this was a big disappointment for the production company, because they really wanted me to re-shoot the scene and to change it, but Protée's refusal was the purpose of the film.

Chantal Akerman

I don't think there is such a thing as European identity. The reasons why this question has arisen are, on one hand, the increasing global domination of Hollywood, and on the other, the existence of the European Community and its ability to put money into European co-productions. The only thing the countries of Europe have in common is their collective guilt in allowing the Nazis to slaughter Europe's Jewish population during the Second World War. For me, cinema is about personal stories. The point behind cinema was to feel that something important has happened, that something new has been experienced.

I decided to make films after I saw *Pierrot le fou*. I realised then that cinema was a language, as strong and fulfilling an experience as litera-ture or painting. I was fifteen at the time, and this was an extra-ordinary experience. I haven't seen the film since and I must admit I'm a bit afraid of doing so. Unfortunately, things are different today. I think it's more difficult for people to open their hearts and minds out to something new than it was in 1965. Most people today are brain-washed by TV.

John Akomfrah

I want to begin by suggesting that part of the problem with a discussion of this nature is that the categories are too big. Europe poses particular problems for someone who is still caught up in trying to argue that to be African *and* British are not mutually exclusive categories. However, I do think that the standpoint I have adopted over the last decade as a black British citizen and film-maker could inform a debate about Europe and European cinema if the terms of the debate were somehow made narrower and more focused.

I'm going to refer to a book by the African-American writer John Edgar Wideman, *Brothers and Keepers*, in which he relates how when he was young he would walk down streets and look at cars, and in his mind he would buy them, but for nickels and dimes. Wideman contrasts the experiences of himself (a middle-class professor of English in a fashionable American university) and his brother (an under-class heroin dealer serving a life sentence, without the possibility of parole, for killing a man in a botched robbery attempt). Essentially, Wideman is confronting the American dream and the American nightmare: two destinies which prefigure as a set of possibilities known and lived through in a culture which changes and charges these two destinies with an intensity unrivalled anywhere else. They are possibilities in the symbolic order made all too real by history and politics, and in many ways are captives of themselves, pinned down by a pincer movement of myth and metaphor on a battlefield which is wholly imaginary, since it's about how identities are formed. But it's also simultaneously real because it's about the social relations through which these identities are constituted.

In this war zone of criss-crossing signs and codes and icons and fantasies, Wideman wants to find a story which is concerned with memory and retrieval. He wants to set in motion a meditation or reflection on cultural values. At the heart of these cultural values he wants to highlight a neatly framed anxiety around power. He attempts to do this through a narrative about cars: who can afford, who can't afford to buy cars, and the symbolic significance of buying cars in a culture which invests the business of buying with the language of humanity – if you buy you can be human. This metaphor unlocks the mystery of power and infuses the book with a series of sentiments which I find have similarities to those contained in the films screened for this conference. The main sentiment is that of a 'double consciousness': a sense of being within while remaining an enforced outsider, so that one brings to the knowledge of being within, experiences of those who were formed on the periphery.

The division between Europe and America, one of the 'others' which organises any discussion about European cinema, isn't a particularly helpful one. I am interested in American cinema as a kind of 'Old Country' (in cultural terms), but not in the sense that I want to propose an opposite 'new country' in the shape of a monolithic European cinema, as this would rob people of the ability to make strategic connections between things which are of value across boundaries and territories and would leave us without some idea of what a possible site of memory could be. If one talks purely about identities and social relations, then my sense of what it is to be black has been formed in negotiation with things profoundly of the new world: the United States, the Caribbean, Cuba and so on, and I certainly don't want to let go of these if this is a precondition to becoming part of a European cinema.

Despite this, I am interested in Europe as a paradigm of cultural possibility. I am interested in the notion of flux, in the shifts which seem to constitute diasporic identity in Europe. And in so far as there is any commitment to European cinema, it is to those things which try to rescue and retrieve flux, possibilities and memory. In my opinion, no film in the programme does this more brilliantly than *Young Soul Rebels*.

Discussion

In the open discussion which followed, Akomfrah was asked if and how *Young Soul Rebels* could revive the memory of resistance in the Caribbean. He replied by citing a play he'd seen which dealt with the pushing out from London's West End of a group of Nigerian underworld figures just after the war, when the British hoods had come back from the fighting and were trying to reassert their rights over space. It struck him that the West End has been precisely that – a battleground over style as well as over who controls the streets. This relates directly to *Young Soul Rebels*: the struggle in that film is in some ways a rerun of earlier struggles.

The session quickly threw up the question of the problems of reaching an audience, which then provoked a discussion about subtitling and dubbing practices in European countries. Because a film like *Chocolat* had been included in the Cannes Film Festival, this gave it a cultural value which meant that it was not dubbed to the same extent it might have been. Claire Denis argued that it was important to fight for subtitles, although this remained almost impossible with regard to certain countries such as Germany and Italy. However, the reasons why some countries tend to dub and others to subtitle foreign-language films were often due to particular historical circumstances.

Films are not dubbed in Portugal, for example, due to a precedent set in the 1950s, when dubbing was too expensive. So, despite being dominated by the Hollywood majors, Portugal subtitles all foreign films. In Italy, on the other hand, dubbing is pervasive because after the war Italian unions demanded dubbing work for their members.

Denis's latest film *S'en fout la mort* features a young man from Martinique, now in Paris, who at one stage decides not to speak French any more but, rather, reverts to French Creole as spoken in Martinique. But this very important aspect was lost in the dubbing process. Consequently, she now insists on a clause in her contract that allows her to insist, in the case of dubbed versions of her films, that a black character be dubbed by a black actor who can understand subtle cultural differences and nuances of language.

Felix De Rooy decided the whole discussion about dubbing and subtitling was xenophobic, a reflection of cultural imperialism and a lack of respect for other languages. He had earlier berated the English and French for their disinclination to learn other languages. Someone from the floor suggested he was missing the point in that it is the language factor which makes it difficult for European films to find a mass audience in the way Hollywood cinema can. This in turn prevents the development of a strong financial base for European film-making.

The relationship between European and American cinema was touched upon in a couple of ways. The American domination of the British market made it extremely difficult for British films to gain access to cinemas. Chantal Akerman pointed out that while some small American films were made, mostly in New York, the majority of US product was essentially the same. She was also pessimistic about the imposition of a television style on European cinema which also serves to produce a similarly stifling conformity among film-makers.

A contradictory European approach to American cinema was identified, manifesting itself as a rejection of American cinema as a negative cultural influence on the one hand, while at the same time incorporating elements of American cinematic technique and style on the other. Felix De Rooy cited the case of a Dutch film called *How to Survive a Broken Heart* which was predominantly in English using American actors. He also made the controversial suggestion that Almodóvar's *Women on the Verge of a Nervous Breakdown* was essentially an American film made in Spanish.

It was pointed out from the floor that European films such as *A bout de souffle* owe much to the American 'B' movie tradition and that if European cinema is to be seen as an oppositional cinema to Hollywood, in cultural terms, then there should be no need to compete on Hollywood's terms, no desire to produce big-budget, mass-market films. That is to say, if small films are its tradition and what Europe does well, then why construct a counter-monolith to compete with the American version? Claire Denis was fearful of the pressures to make bigger, more commercial films which would interest, for example a famous German actor, or to compromise by making such a film in the English language. She also commented on American film companies buying the rights to remake certain European films such as *Women on the Verge* (*Three Men and a Baby* is another recent example), which tend to be comedies. European cinema in this sense could be seen as an experiment which American executives watched closely to see if films work, and if they do, they turn them into something else. Chantal Akerman ended the session by suggesting that although she had always made small films, this was only one way of doing things and that European cinema could produce many different films of different sizes. A small budget doesn't necessarily result in a 'B' movie.

FINAL PANEL OF RESPONDENTS
Introduction

Colin MacCabe

There are a few moments in one's life when one has a certain notion of the fitness of things, and I must admit these last two days have been one of them. For the last two years, we've been engaged at the BFI in trying to produce a new kind of mix of theory and practice, and to put together the various resources of the Institute in a way which would make for new kinds of intellectual combinations. This event, with the programme of films, with the variety of forms of address and speaker, and indeed with the participation of both Jean-Luc Godard and the BFI's own production *Young Soul Rebels*, makes this a very satisfying moment.

On an autobiographical note, I must also say that the cinema for me is not a life-long passion. As a teenager, British television offered me much more interest than anything I could see at the cinemas I went to, except possibly the NFT. But at the age of seventeen, I had the same kind of experience that happened to Chantal Akerman (who had talked about the momentous effect that seeing Godard's *Pierrot le fou* had had on her, the experience which had inspired her to become a film-maker). I had gone to Paris for the first time and I went to see a film called *Made in the USA*, which I assumed, rather ignorantly, would be in English. In fact, only one bit of it was in English: Marianne Faithfull singing 'As Tears Go By'. But it was the first time in the cinema I saw something which I really thought I hadn't seen before, and it's from that moment that I became interested in cinema. It is therefore always a privilege for me to talk with and to Jean-Luc Godard.

But I do have to say that, great as his performance was last night, I fundamentally disagree with him on almost every point he made. In particular, when he said that what he wished was that on television you could see some bad Greek films, some bad Dutch films as well as some bad American ones, I felt like interrupting and saying, 'Well, Jean-Luc, for the last three or four years, that's what a lot of us have been engaged in doing.' In particular, I had quite a lot to do with a scheme called the European Film Distribution Office (EFDO), which is entirely devoted to making sure it's possible to see more bad European films in European countries. And I was also quite serious when I said at the beginning of last night that the questions we pose ourselves about Europe here are really very important and vital ones for me. They're not an accident. America, for me, in that sense, is a very late addition. I put down deposits for tickets in 1968, 1969 and 1970, but I never got there until 1981. But Europe is, for me, very much a reality.

Until I was fifteen I thought I was Irish. I then realised I wasn't that, but at the same time I knew I wasn't English. It was really only in that moment, in going to Paris at the end of my teens, I realised that if I was anything, I was European. And I must say that I'd always felt very comfortable with that identity in its miscegenated, hybrid form, in the form London in the 1960s gave me. Then in the winter of 1989 I suddenly realised I wasn't a European, I was a west European. As we were planning this conference, there was a horrible moment in January when I suddenly realised that through error, omission or whatever, we'd made a real mistake in that we didn't have a voice from eastern Europe. And then I realised that in addition to that lack, we also didn't have anybody from southern Europe. We had Almodóvar's film, but we didn't have anybody from Italy, one of the great film-making countries.

But a solution to this problem was close at hand. My life is also split between the British Film Institute and Pittsburg University in America, and I realised that Pittsburg could solve my problem directly, so I invited Vladimir Padunov and Nancy Condee from the Slavic Studies Department, and Patrizia Lombardo from the Italian and French Department. And then it struck me that, although we would have various voices commenting on the issues and questions at hand, in the end the great buzz concept in academia is the global, and so we needed a global perspective. And there's really only one person I can think of who could provide such a perspective, and that's Fredric Jameson of Duke University, North Carolina.

Responses

Nancy Condee

I want to return to the issue of European cartography that we talked about briefly this morning, in particular the question of Eastern Europe and the Soviet Union. What struck me about much of the discussion was its profoundly Eurocentric nature. There is nothing wrong, *per se*, with discussing European culture from a Eurocentric perspective, but valuable alternatives do exist and need to be recognised. Just as a discussion of heterosexuality need not necessarily be framed in terms of a heterosexual perspective, or patriarchy from a patriarchial perspective, or US culture from an Ameriocentric perspective, so toò it is possible to talk about definitions of Europe from some perspective other than what we normally conceive of as European. I was also appalled by many things Jean-Luc Godard said last night, in particular the reduction of Russian culture to Dostoyevsky and *Battleship Potemkin*, and the complete absence of any acknowledgement that Eastern Europe existed at all.

I have a rather simple definition of Europe, which I'm very happy to either defend further or, in the face of compulsive alternative conceptions, to capitulate and change my mind. My definition of Europe stops at the Urals; until then, it's all Europe to me. That is not to say that there isn't differentiation, but I don't necessarily recognise the 'Western Europe' and 'Other Europe' distinction. Within the latter there is so much heterogeneity that the whole notion of 'other Europe' is merely a kind of convenience that doesn't have a lot of substance to it.

Another thing I found quite puzzling about Godard's statements was the distinction, maintained throughout his formative years, that he was taught not that Lenin was a great revolutionary, but that Goethe was a great writer. This is an opposition that, particularly in Eastern Europe, doesn't fit as comfortably for generations who were brought up to believe that Lenin can be a great revolutionary *and* Goethe can be a great writer, and further, that the undoing of this involves a much greater complexity. The peoples of Eastern Europe have a very different relationship to that so-called opposition from those of us who grew up in the West. What I'm trying to suggest is that, in discussing 'European' culture and 'European' cinema, it helps to place the question in dialogue not only in relation to the United States, but also with the East. What I would like to do in focusing on this issue is to restrict myself for the moment to notions of mainstream cinema, and in particular mainstream cinema in the Soviet Union, which is my area of specialisation.

Within the discussion of mainstream cinema there are three issues in particular which help to redefine a notion of European cinema. The first has to do with sexuality. In contradistinction to the United States, where sexuality in Hollywood cinema tends to be a kind of patriarchial sanitised-heterosexuality, we have, in contemporary mainstream Soviet cinema, a less sanitised version of heterosexuality which relates more closely to the concerns of European cinema. I'm thinking here of

74

such film-makers as Kira Muratova, Sergei Solovoyov, or Pavel Lungin. The audience to whom they are speaking, in their exploration of different kinds of hetereosexuality and the representation of heterosexuality, is a different audience from that addressed by their American counterparts. (The issue of homosexuality is a much more complex one because of an abiding homophobia in Soviet culture as a whole.)

The second point I want to call attention to in defining European culture has to do with politics. In contemporary mainstream Soviet cinema there is a kind of ironic, savage concern for 'post-Marxism'. This concern clearly comes out of the experience of a failed Marxism-Leninism, not as an ideology but as a lived experience, and encounters a more comprehending public in Europe than it does in the United States. The response to the fall of Communism, as it has been formulated in the United States, has been approximately this: 'We were right all along; we already knew this; we didn't have to go through the crashing and burning of Communism to see that it was a flop.' The dialogue that is taking place in the Soviet Union about what happened to Marxism is more investigative than that. Consequently, if we are looking for some kind of a definition of European culture, its relationship to Marxism is definitely one of the aspects worth examining.

The third issue has to do with economics. Examinations of contemporary mainstream Soviet cinema – its earliest attempts at *perestroika*, its revisionist *perestroika*, and its third commercial *perestroika*; its convulsive attempts to find a model of cultural production that suits its newly emerging economic relations; the joint ventures with Western Europe and the reworking of Western models – all these constitute a more appropriate search than one directed towards the vast Hollywood superstructure. Hollywood, for Soviet film-makers, is a wet dream. As Soviet culture goes through a process of decentralisation, not only in political but also in cultural terms, its search for models founded on Western European culture is much more productive than a search for American models. To return to some kind of groping definition of European culture, the kinds of economic models found in Western Europe allow a more appropriate posing of the question.

Finally, let me turn briefly away from mainstream cinema to alternative cinema. If we can say that alternative cinema in the West is often concerned with issues of gender, feminism, sexual preference, the marginalisation of ethnic identities, leftist politics and Marxism-Leninism, we find in Soviet alternative cinema virtually none of these concerns. If anything we find an antipathy to such issues. Instead, we find a concern with rock culture and youth culture, cultural hooliganism; in particular (oddly enough), issues of necrophilia (which is a

75

much more popular topic than homophilia in Soviet alternative cinema) and a concern with formal issues, specifically the dismantling of the totalitarian aesthetic of socialist realism. In that respect, alternative Soviet cinema is not all that distinct from mainstream Soviet cinema: both are concerned with the shared repudiation of the past, a repudiation of Stalinist aesthetics. Therefore, Godard's definition of cinema as 'white boys from industrial countries' is precisely, I think, what much of Soviet cinema aspires to, whether alternative or mainstream. If one is going to be fastidious about one's political correctness, one is in big trouble dealing with the Soviet Union, yet it provides a valuable perspective in such a discussion about European culture and European cinema.

Vladimir Padunov

As a balance to Nancy's attempt, in speaking from the 'other Europe', to open up an integrative dialogue, I'm going to take the disintegrative approach. I'll begin by pointing out that the words 'imperialism' and 'colonialism' have come up several times in this conference. I would rather begin with the words 'empire' and 'imperial aspiration', and point out that the Soviet empire, or more accurately the Russian empire, differs from the classic model of modern empire (which is a nice oxymoron) if by 'modern empire' we specifically have in mind the European imperial states. These states, as opposed to the Romanov empire, were specially reconstituted. They were not geo-integrated but, rather, were dispersed; they implicated, by definition, multiple means of transport. You could not move across the empire on four-legged beasts, whether horse or camel, because neither could cross the ocean. In the classical model, colony is always 'over there'. I don't question the notion of 'there', but I do question what stands under the word 'over'. Under the 'over', invariably, is a body of water.

The Romanov empire differs in this respect: it is an essentially landlocked empire. You move, not from one means of land transport to boat or plane and then back again, but rather, you simply move from horse to camel and then back to horse. It is interesting that the classic model of modern empire begins to dismantle once air transport begins to generate the false seamlessness of geographic relocation. The Romanov empire essentially is bordered on the west by the Hanseatic states, the Baltics; on the south by the Transcaucasus, which are themselves problematic, the Asian expanses of the five central Asian republics, and Siberia. Consequently, the centre is never centred in the Russian empire. Earlier this afternoon, I talked about the 'sunset centrism' of this conference. I would like to point out that this same point can be made about the Russian empire: it has always been decentred, in that its centres are located at the western periphery of the empire – Leningrad and Moscow.

So we begin with a decentred centre when we look at the Russian empire and at the constitution of national identity. What that does (and we tend not to notice this) is to redefine the function of the periphery in constituting the cultural identity located in the centre. The best example of this fact in the history of Soviet cinema can be found in the status, for example, of the film studios in Kirgizia and Kazakhstan. Kirgizfilm and Kazakhfilm began to emerge in the second half of the 1960s and early 1970s as an alternative to the cultural identity being imposed by the central film industries. These include Mosfilm (Moscow Film Studio, the largest in the Soviet Union); Lenfilm in Leningrad; and the Gorky Film Studio in the Ukraine. Kirgizfilm and Kazakhfilm were able to resist the homogenised cultural identity that was completely official, but paradoxically this opposition was led by completely official film-makers in that film-makers from Mosfilm would go to Kirgizia and Kazakhstan to make their 'alternative cinema'.

This group included Larissa Shepitko, the late wife of Elem Klimov, Andrei Konchalovsky (whose name used to be Andron Mikhalkov Konshalovsky before he moved to Hollywood), Nikita Mikhalkov, his half-brother who is increasingly seen in the Soviet Union as a Western rather than a Soviet film-maker, and many others. The classic popular film of this period is *Trans-Siberian Express*, a kind of Soviet *Stagecoach* with a slant-eyed John Wayne. It is a cross between the American detective film, the American western, the American spy film and the picaresque novel – the journey of education.

Interestingly enough, Kirgizfilm and Kazakhfilm have re-emerged in the period of *glasnost* and *perestroika*. A special seminar was held at the Moscow Film Institute (VGIK) under Sergei Solov'ev (the director of films like *Red Rose, Black Rose* and *Assa*) at which a small group of very young Kazakh film-makers were enrolled. One of them was Rashid Nugmanov, who is now head of the union of film-makers in Kazakhstan. Immediately after Nugmanov returned to Kazakhfilm, he made his now famous film *The Needle*. This film, too, was based on foreign cinematic models, but in this case European (specifically the European version of film noir) rather than American. Nugmanov also used Soviet musicians (Petr Mamonov of the rock group Zvukimu and Viktor Tsoi, the lead singer of Kino) rather than actors. In other words, counter-cultural identity was used as a filmic centre by a film studio existing in opposition to the political–cultural centre.

The current debate in Soviet cinema is quite different from that in Western cinema. The debate there is between the relative merits of *avorskoe kino* – the closest you can come to defining this term is auteur cinema, although it means substantially more than that because the category of 'art cinema' does not exist in the Soviet Union – and *kommercheskoe kino*, or commercial cinema. Commercial cinema in the Soviet Union is invariably based on the American model and includes films that you will probably never see in this country such as *Pirates of the Twentieth Century*, *Solo Voyage* and *The Blonde around the Corner*. Such films are massively popular with Soviet audiences.

This debate has led to the restructuring of the entire film production industry in the Soviet Union, beginning in 1986: the reorganising of the Union of Cinematographers and its relationship to the State Committee on Cinematography (Goskino), and the reconstituting of all the film studios. However, all of this restructuring has failed to help contemporary film-makers, because what has never been taken into account in the Soviet Union are problems of film distribution. For example, according to Soviet newspapers, in the week of 28 April through to 4 May 1991 there were 312 films being screened in Moscow. That includes film theatres, houses of leisure, palaces of culture, the Union of Cinematographers, factories and underground videocassette halls. Of these 312 films only twenty-two were Soviet produced. Of these twenty-two, nineteen were Russian, one was Georgian, one was Kazakh, and one was from the Baltic republics. Most of the remaining 290 films wouldn't qualify as 'B' grade movies. They include *The Battle of the Amazons*, *The Return of the Ninja* and *Hot Target* – in other words, American movies purchased by the Soviet distribution Mafia headed by a man called Ismail Tagi-Zade, an Azeri cowboy complete with white suit and stetson, who flew four planeloads (this in hard currency!) of Soviet representatives to Cannes for the festival, where he had rented an entire hotel. Tagi-Zade now controls the majority of film-viewing places in Moscow and has declared that he is about to take Soviet cinema off the Soviet screens.

The question then that has to be posed here in the West is, 'what role does cinema play in constituting national identity at the centre?' The question, however, is not worded in this way in Moscow. The debate in the Soviet Union is between culture (and they claim that they do have a culture) and civilisation, by which they simply mean West European civility, which they claim they do not have. What is interesting in the debate is the contradiction between the ability to integrate *emigré* literary traditions (Nabokov and the entire diaspora of Russian-language literature produced in emigration), and the concomitant inability to integrate *emigré* film production and cultural history – for example, Slava Tsuckerman's *Liquid Sky*, or even the films of Konchalovsky, which are not considered part of Soviet cinema.

78

In conclusion, I want to point out that the determining factor in the debate between culture and civility in the Soviet Union at the moment comes down to the problem of national identity. Identity has been invoked here repeatedly; it has been invoked too frequently as an already existing entity. I would agree with one of the earlier speakers: it is specifically the production and distribution of narratives that forms identity; identity is something that is always in the process of being formed. It never exists in the present because it is constituted by a specific relationship to the past. And if there is no relationship to the past, in effect if there is no past, then it is premature to talk about identity. The Soviet Union is unique at the moment in that it is perhaps the only country with a determined present and an absolutely undetermined past.

Patrizia Lombardo

I do not know if my perspective here will be exactly Mediterranean, as Colin suggested, but it will certainly be European, in a Weberian sense, because it considers what are inextricably European phenomena: the big city, modernity and the emergence of the philosophy of modernity out of the metropolitan experience. My major reference points here are Max Weber's *The European City*, Georg Simmel's *Philosophy of Modernity* and Walter Benjamin's essay 'On Some Motifs in Baudelaire' which formed part of his study of nineteenth-century Paris. I believe that the idea of post-colonialism, which has been central to this conference, should be seen in relation to those metropolitan crowds which so fascinated Benjamin and which had such an effect on the imagination of observers from Engels, to Poe, to Hugo, to Baudelaire. And I would argue that the mass media – advertisements, cinema, television, video – in serving to structure our perceptions of reality, also constitute an extension of the experience of the nineteenth-century metropolis, which had fulfilled a similar role in shaping the perceptions of its inhabitants. Benjamin, for example, talks about how the sheer quantity and multiplicity of stimuli and impressions served to atrophy experience: the more consciousness was bombarded by impressions, the more it has to internalise the shocks of the external world in order to protect the self from their traumatic effects.

Today we face the fact of post-colonialism in much the same way that people faced the huge crowds of Paris or London. We begin by developing a language appropriate for describing post-colonialism; for theorising its complexities in terms of migrant identities, subaltern discourse, global perspectives, decentred centres and demarginalised margins. We have started to integrate perceptions of this post-colonial reality into the ways in which we ask certain questions, organise curricula, document contemporary life, perceive political processes in terms of new themes and new objects of investigation. In this regard, I think of just how right Marx was when he said that it's much easier to be philosophical contemporaries of ourselves than historical contemporaries, in that historical events, at the very moment they occur, often destroy our ideas, our theories and the progress we attributed to them.

We have witnessed the decolonisation of parts of the world. The effects of this are visible in the form of the presence of Algerians, Moroccans and Tunisians in Paris, and of Jamaicans, Pakistanis and Indians in London. However, when considering the rather problematic question of cultural identity in relation to these patterns of post-colonial migration, we have to go beyond any simple question of cultural or ethnic origin. We have to take on board, as Stuart Hall put it, the question of hybridity, the network of integration and resistance that maps the identity of young second- or third-generation immigrants. I am thinking, in this respect, of Gurinder Chadha's documentary *I'm British But ...*, produced by the BFI, which examines the experience of young Asians born and brought up in Britain. I am also thinking of the phenomena of some contemporary rock music, reggae music and African music where this idea of hybridity is identifiably at work with its creative, post-modern glimmers. Only blinkered conservatives refuse to see all of this, as some conservatives refused to acknowledge the significance of the metropolis in the nineteenth century and instead sought shelter in the nostalgic myth of nature.

So while we do have some philosophical grasp of post-colonialism, what we don't have (and this seems to be evident in the debates of this conference) is a language which enables us to talk about the recent events, and the changes taking place, in Eastern Europe. We can report the events, express our hopes and our fears, but we cannot quite grasp their historical significance. The moment in which history is made somehow evades our analytical tools.[1] Consequently, we are at present somewhat silent in the face of recent events in Eastern Europe. What language can we use to describe what has happened? Can we still talk about Marxism or liberalism or market economies? Can we rely on the old sets of oppositions? How do we deal with a global perspective when we are only too aware that people are killing each other in the name of national identity? How do we reconcile our computer-age, post-modern understandings with conflicts which appear rooted in the nineteenth century?

I don't have answers to these questions, but what I want to do is raise the issue Stuart Hall touched upon this morning: what is this enigma that Europe poses for itself and for others? I for one have never understood Europe in terms of a mode of film production which is opposed to an American mode of film production. Rather, I have understood Europe in terms of an image given or projected by the kind of films we have seen for this conference. I recognise its presence as an endeavour, a mass of myths, ideologies, fictions, resistances and projects. But in this sense of an interplay between a physical space and the set of discourses and activities which give that space an imaginary reality, I would categorically oppose any Eurocentric perspective. I would argue that, with respect to contemporary post-colonial Europe, any centralising discourse is as regressive as the nineteenth-century nostalgia for nature and physiocratic modes of production and human relationships. But the puzzle of Europe remains, mitigating within frontiers and beyond oceans, in a continuous work of composition and decomposition, composed of fragments we put together in a design which resists smoothness and uniformity.

However, there are themes which help us to make sense of the contemporary realities of this post-colonial Europe, and I should like to identify some of them here. One theme I have already invoked is that of hybridity. This is a question of having several identities; a puzzle central to the idea of European identity. Felix De Rooy was saying earlier that outside forces have always existed in the European context. This has been the reality of the European city since the Middle Ages. Max Weber, for example, defines the city as a versatile economic reality founded on commercial rather than agricultural activity, composed of different social classes and (significantly) open to processes of immigration and circulation of inhabitants who came to recognise themselves as belonging not to a family or clan, but as individual citizens in an administrative unit. The Italian historian Carlo Ginzburg has demonstrated that many Italian folk tales from the Middle Ages had Asian rather than Christian origins. This demonstrates a migratory movement of short stories and legends beyond any narrow cultural 'belonging'. Consequently, there is no pure Judeo-Christian identity because other identities have impacted upon it, transforming its substance in the process.

The second theme which I think is very important is that of migration. As Stuart Hall pointed out, the native population in some of the big cities of Europe is actually in the minority, making these, in a sense, Third World cities. I think that this fact should be rigorously examined using a combination of the techniques of demographic research, statistics and sociology as instruments of social and political analysis.[2]

The questions of hybridity and migration lead to another theme, again raised by Stuart: that of being polyglot, both literally and metaphorically. Being polyglot doesn't simply mean the ability to speak several languages. It relates to the experience of living in a perennial state of non-determination, lingering in the interregnum of speaking and not speaking, of understanding and not understanding. In that sense I'm a great supporter of Europe, because I adore is multiplicity of languages, dialects, voices, tones and inflections which have always undermined the bogus purity of a concept of national identity.

There is a fourth theme which I would like to add, that of the interplay between the local and the international. This interplay also means the reconstitution of Europe, beyond national boundaries, as a map of regional subcultures. The term 'local', as I understand it, only has meaning in relation to the term 'international': it cannot be reduced to folklore, to a sort of native genuineness. The local indicates a physical space where history has accumulated with a multitude of memories and oblivions.

Let me take the example of the film *Time of the Gypsies*. This had all the elements of a folkloristic film with its turkeys, Gypsies, magic and superstitions. And yet it overcame simple folklore; the scene became international, moving from the outskirts of Ljubljana into Ljubljana itself and then on to Milan and Rome. The film both proposes marginality in the centre and explores the interplay of marginality and centre. The Gypsies from Ljubljana are seen at work in the centre of Milan, they meet in the Piazza Navona in Rome, or they hide their loot under an old stone of a very central street in old Milan. These are very powerful images for me.

I would also argue that *Time of the Gypsies* transcended folklore at the level of technique. The film moves from the apparently slow world of the Gypsy community on the outskirts of the city into the much quicker pace of metropolitan life, with the head Gypsy periodically returning to his village to recruit new labour. The community of wandering Gypsies inhabit a bizarre underworld, living in trailers in a devastated urban–suburban landscape of wasteground set against a backdrop of a highway bridge. The film combines images of the almost agrarian setting of the Gypsy village with those of an urban environment straight out of an American film.[3] In narrative terms *Time of the Gypsies* echoes the chronology, centred around traditional rites of passage, of *The Godfather*. The scene towards the end of the wedding in Rome recalls the first scene in Coppola's film. The rhythm of the narrative is quick, the build-up in suspense prepares us for the final vendetta with its outbursts of blood and violence. How far removed this tragic climax is from the initial scenes in which we are introduced to the rhythms of daily life in the Gypsy settlement. Kusturica's film, therefore, is a generic hybrid of social documentary and the American crime film, successfully fusing modes of realism with the fantastic and in way which reminds me of Gabriel Garciá Márquez's literary masterpiece of hybridity, *One Hundred Years of Solitude*, which fuses realism and surrealism, myth and history.

Now we may embrace this idea of Europe as a multicultural reality, but we also have to comprehend the simultaneous dissolution of national boundaries in Western Europe together with the emergence of old nationalist claims in the East, which we thought had been buried in the past. We should understand, as Philip Dodd pointed out, that that post-colonialism is not the end of colonialism as such because there are new colonialisms emerging. Rather, what we need is a new understanding, a rereading of the old colonialism, and the breaking of it. Here again I would return to the idea of the big city, as Benjamin saw it, as the site of hybridity, of migration, of many languages – the continuation of which, in terms of their rhythms and quickness, is the world of information systems and the mass media.

Benjamin does speak a lot about techniques: how they effect our consciousness and our reception of the art object. As I have already indicated, I think the question of technique is very important, and in this sense I would like to speak very briefly about some recent Italian films, which I would describe as hybrids simultaneously transgressing and absorbing a so-called Italian filmic tradition.[4] A great deal of recent Italian cinema can be seen in terms of a mixture of American film technique and indigenous Italian characteristics. (Being Italian is a very good starting-point in being European because one never feels that one is simply Italian. There is no one Italian national identity, but rather many local and regional identities.) Let me give you some examples.

One film which springs to mind is *Americano Rosso*, by Alessandro D'Alatri. D'Alatri comes from the world of advertising like Chatillez in France (the director of that incredible satire of bourgeois family life *La Vie est un long fleuve tranquille*). This move from advertising to cinema obviously implies certain questions of technique. The sketch-book aesthetics of advertising (immediately identifiable in *Americano Rosso*, as the title of the film is the name of a cocktail) gives a comic gloss to the narrative which ostensibly deals with everyday life in a provincial town in Veneto during Fascism. The Fascism portrayed is ideologically weak but pervasive, socially inscribed in terms of *petit-bourgeois* mediocrity: a small wedding agency, the respectability of a Grand Hotel life, and a slumbering lagoon landscape. D'Alatri breaks with the most stereotyped modes of representing Fascism, either in terms of a caricature of the oppressors or the strength of the anti-Fascist opposition. Rather, he presents an Italy which is slowly and gradually sinking into consensus.

What is interesting about D'Alatri is the way in which he makes a

83

break from the Italian tradition of the *film d'autore*, where you had total auteurs, like the Italian greats of the 50s and 60s, who did everything in relation to the film-making process: screenplay, direction, and editing. In contrast, D'Alatri is only the director, the screenplay is by Enzo Monteleone, who adapted his script from the novel of the same title by Gino Pugnetti. As Roberto Escobar wrote in his review of *Americano Rosso* in *Il Sole–24 Ore*, D'alatri concentrated his creative energies exclusively on the translation of literary images into filmic images. He is an expert of the image, not a high priest of the total work of art. His narrative technique is that of the American thriller: he disrupts the chronology of real time by condensing and manipulating it in order to heighten the impact of the narrative on the viewer. At the same time the emotional orientation of the film is firmly located in Italian history (in particular the disturbing consensus of Fascism in the 30s) and Italian folklore.

In comparison with D'Alatri's approach to cinema, you have a film like Tornatore's *Cinema Paradiso*, which was extremely successful in the United States and elsewhere. This film represents a nostalgic Italy, as far removed from contemporary Italian cultural reality as pizza and spaghetti. Here you have this little Sicilian village, which is poor but honest, a stark contrast with the corruption of the big city, in this case Rome. You have the young boy who was so happy when he lived in the village where he knew sincere love and friendship, who then grows up, moves to Rome and becomes a rich and famous film director, has many women, but yet is unhappy, yearning for the life he left behind. This folklorist nostalgia for childhood and a more simple, traditional existence is the classic conservative response to the experience of modernity.

There is one moment in the film which has a potentially real poetic value, that being the final film within a film composed of the footage of love-scenes from American movies which had been censored by the village priest. But the fragmentary poetics of the scene are undercut by its positioning in the narrative – after the cathartic return to the village, when we find that the movie house has been destroyed. This fixes it as a sort of nostalgic compensation: the sweetness of memory making up for the disappointment and loss of the present.

Another film I should like to talk about is *Ultra*, an example of the emergence of a new kind of Italian cinema. I think one can talk about a new *nouvelle vague* of film-makers; a generation which grew up in the late 60s. As Roberto Escobar has argued, this generation are questioning and interrogating the European enigma which I mentioned earlier. They are asking the same questions as Isaac Julien asked himself with *Young Soul Rebels*: what stories to tell, where to situate these stories in space and time, how to tell these stories, and deciding which existing modes of storytelling to follow and where there is a need for the creation of new modes.

The director of *Ultra*, Ricky Tognazzi, deals in original filmic ideas, with no previous literary text as a starting point. He reads and interprets the world through images, in the way a mathematician thinks in figures or a musician in sounds. Some critics have categorised *Ultra* as neo neo-realism, demonstrating the need to find a label, to relate something to tradition or the reworking of a tradition.

The film tells the story of a group of hooligans who journey from Rome to Turin for a big football match. It presents a kind of Italy which traditionalists don't like: an urban Italy which is very much against the construction of 'Paisa' (the peasant Italy informing *Cinema Paradiso*), which Pasolini also undermined in his film *Accatone*. In this respect *Ultra* returns me to my earlier theme of the metropolis. The metropolitan Italy it represents is violent and ruthless. You are never shown the football match, only the hooligans, the trains, the streets, the desolate space under the stadium. The violence is so deeply rooted that it transcends issues of right-wing or left-wing ideology, it is neither exalted nor condemned.

Moreover, the narration is broken into elipses, illusions and continuous montage. The film does not attempt to reconstruct real time like neo-realism, but rather it concentrates, manipulates and falsifies time in the way American films do. Again, what we have is a hybrid of American technique and an inspiration which relates back to Pasolini and his insights into marginal experience produced by the metropolis. However, the major difference between Tognazzi and Pasolini is that the latter analyses metropolitan marginality as almost an internal or mythical phenomenon, while Tognazzi externalises things and events in the brutality of existence and in the vertiginous scansion of time.

Another point I should like to make here concerns language. We have talked a lot about language at this conference and we have heard the variety of languages, voices and accents which Isaac Julien has used in *Your Soul Rebels*. The language of Tognazzi's film is a very difficult one for many Italians since it utilises a very strong Roman dialect and street slang, the hooligans' jargon if you like. There is no folkloristic recuperation of Roman speech, what the romantics would have called the 'local chromatism'. In this instance we have found an effective way of speaking against the official language. The speech in the film, like the narrative structure, is broken, cut and elliptical.

The final scene is particularly breathtaking. This takes place in the basement of the football stadium, which is completely devastated, inundated by dirt and water coming out of pipes and sewers. One of the young hooligans is holding a friend who is dying, accidently stabbed by one of his own group during the scuffle in the stadium.

Here you have the image of terrible metropolitan devastation which tells us that the metropolis is the reality we must face. We cannot afford to shed tears for the loss of a quasi-idyllic agrarian society, like the one proposed by *Cinema Paradiso*. The big city, with its crowds and its migrating identities, is, in fact, the site of the defeat of reason.

Notes

1. Yet it is true to say that some people had foreseen much of what was to occur in the Soviet Union and Eastern Europe. For example, Altiero Spinelli, the Italian anti-Fascist and Communist who was Deputy in the European Parliament in Strasbourg in the 70s, predicted the nationalist tensions currently blighting Eastern Europe. He also foresaw the contradictions which have arisen between the two Europes in that at the moment one Europe would finally overcome the nationalist perspective, the other would be tormented by nationalist upheavals.
2. I believe that the deconstructionist attitude vis-à-vis academic disciplines is somewhat old-fashioned and outmoded. It meant a radical questioning of the status of disciplines which in its pure form, I would argue, corresponds to a 'Luddite' position in that one doesn't free oneself from capitalism simply by destroying machines, but one can attempt to use machines without being dominated by their logics. I am more interested in the use of analytical techniques than with the continuous, and almost self-congratulatory, undermining of their status. In this way I think film can teach us a great deal since it constitutes a rereading of the world through a particular set of techniques. Such techniques allow migrations since they do not have an essential nature, but rather a functional activity, and functions can be changed, adjusted, substituted and perverted.
3. I speak here from a position unashamedly in favour of American cinema. Europeans need to remind themselves constantly of the lessons they can learn from American film techniques.
4. I do not agree with Godard's assertion that there is no Swedish film, only Swedish film-makers. Perhaps, in the moment the film is produced, the major condition of its production is the combination of the creative authorial figure of the film-maker and of a collective work that disrupts the national identity. Nevertheless, the reception of a given film is, or has been, subject to processes which serve to categorise it under a national definition which alludes to a specific film-making tradition. If I talk about Italian neo-realism, for example, the definition may have its deficiencies in relation to the actual heterogeneity of films brought together under the concept of neo-realism, but it remains a useful reference nevertheless.

Fredric Jameson

I'm going to begin with the premise that Europe, and everything associated with it, is not necessarily a good thing, regardless of what

86

one's feelings are regarding the idea of nationalism. Indeed, I think it can be argued that the great casualty of the past few years has not been socialism, which will fatally rear its head again whenever the costs and burdens of capitalism become too onerous, but rather the idea of federation. This idea is dependent on one or more of three conditions. Firstly, the external menace or threat of a unified outside power to a range of different, and even possibly unrelated, communities. Secondly, the confederated union must have a unique chance at some new historical situation or role, which it would be reductive to think of purely in economic terms, although these are the most convenient shorthand. In other words, it has to spring into a void and fill some new geo-political function. Finally, on that more imponderable level of superstructures and of ideology, the federation must correspond to some ideal beyond itself. Gabriel García Márquez's novel *The Labyrinth of the General*, which is about Bolivar's last days and the failure of the whole Latin American Federation, is a kind of meditation on this problem.

At any rate, only idealistic liberals can imagine that people federate for the intrinsic beauties of community and federation itself. Rather, they federate for religion, or, in our time, for socialism, as in the case of the USSR and Yugoslavia. I doubt if they federate for reasons of national or ethnic affinity, unless these are intensified into a vision of religious community or social transformation. And I scarcely think they ever federate simply because they think nationalism is a bad thing.

Yet such anti-nationalism is what was in the air at the end of the Second World War, when the contradictory Hitlerian imperial project was, oddly, thought of as nationalist. Consequently, a systematic attack was mounted on nationalisms in general. You may recall a famous photography exhibition called 'The Family of Man'. It's worth looking a little more closely at this very ambiguous ideological strategy, this kind of anti-nationalism, for which the opposite of the bad nation-state might either be the good federation, or the good non-nationalistic multinational corporation. Obviously these two opposites are not the same thing.

For a deeper insight into these matters, I'm indebted to a stunning essay by Terence Hawkes on T. S. Eliot. In one of the great interpretive acts, Hawkes reads Eliot's career as a kind of stalking horse for NATO. The Peasants thumping about melodiously under the London Blitz in *Four Quartets* are the sop which he thinks Eliot throws to English nationalism; while the larger frame of Eliot's new values, from Virgil and Dante all the way to Paul Valéry, open up a Europe in which (or so the ideological promise runs) England will preserve its individuality and not be swallowed up by aliens and continentals. The crucial thing, of course, is that it is an American who is suggesting this greater cosmopolitanism, and the operation is clearly repeated on a political, economic and military level with the formation of the NATO alliance and, subsequently, the European commonwealth.

But why do the Americans want a European commonwealth? One reason surely has to do with the North American supremacy in the two great areas of food and mass culture, in which an otherwise highly industrialised Europe – or Japan, for that matter – can scarcely compete. I won't attempt to answer this interesting question but merely to use it to suggest that a European idea of American origin isn't really very attractive to Europeans, at least in the long run.

But then again, I don't think the other elements of the Eliot idea can be very attractive either. Older notions of Europe, up to and including his, were staged almost exclusively around two values, sometimes united, sometimes not, namely Christianity and Classicism (the Romans masquerading as Greeks). Surely both of these transnational ideas are dead today, and the high culture which still tries to appeal to them (as in the various multilingual literary reviews that have sprung up in the last year or so) has all the stuffiness of *Encounter* magazine after the war which didn't need the revelation of its CIA financing to display its essential intellectual vacuousness and cultural bankruptcy. In fact, I begin to wonder whether Modernism itself, as an idea and as an ideology, is not coterminous with Europe, and should be judged in much the same way.

The relationship between this kind of Europe and the films we've seen here is a complicated one. I hope I've shown that the concept of Europe is not a positive one that these films could in any way promote or illustrate. Yet they all do emerge in a transnational space in which even overt messages of localism are at once transformed into universal ideas of some kind, if only by the international and festival publics they are of necessity forced to address. I think that these films neither promote some idea of Europe, nor do they attack one. Rather, they operate to repress those features of the European idea which are unacceptable, so as to be in a position to live with the rest of the already given European situation. And I think that two forms of such cosmetic repression can be detected here.

The first has to do with language. Despite the world primacy of American English, the European idea has to negotiate the impossible situation of multiple languages in which no new lingua franca or trancendental Joycean pidgin is available. This is already registered in *Passion*, where all the characters have this or that speech defect: stuttering, coughing, 'multisme', heavy accents and so on, and all of this very pointedly in the absence of English as such, since Jerzy will not go to America. But the dilemma of Babel can also be addressed in another way: namely, by displacing the sensory centre of gravity from speech to sight. Indeed, I think one of the striking features of world cinematographic production today is the extraordinary libidinal investment in the image and in sight, in such a way as to downplay or repress the problem of languages. I would argue that even music today is essentially visual, as in the case of MTV. So the new visual aestheticism, of which Jarman and Godard are very different exemplars, functions in the European context as a way of distracting us from this problem of many languages, which would otherwise generate the Freudian anxiety of an unpleasant memory of the dominance of the United States and its hegemonic commercial language, sometimes also called English.

The second form of repression is that shell game in which we are distracted from the fact of the nation-state by that other, seemingly related but very different, fact called 'ethnicity' or 'marginality'. Beginning historically with the holocaust industry, and then moving across a range of racial, ethnic and gender minorities, contemporary film, as clearly in some of those we have seen here, can repress the problem of the still hegemonic nation-state, with its ruling classes and power systems, but focusing instead on the social pluralisms of the new post-60s EC realities with their migrant workers, new social movements and multiracial populations. I'm not suggesting that these struggles are not real and urgent ones in their own national contexts, but rather that, in the European context, the message of this or that local struggle becomes instead the advertisement for some universally tolerant late-capitalism pluralism and democracy. The solidarity of the various marginalities in their isolated struggles of whatever kind then projects some spurious European federation of the minorities on to the propaganda screen, and diverts attention from the other more sinister mergers that work in Europe today, if only because the marginalities, virtually by definition, can never be unified in some federal way, and surely do not want to be.

The crucial exhibit here is, of course, the centrepiece of the whole filmic series, namely Isaac Julien's *Young Soul Rebels*: a kind of historical film which strategically returns to a year (1977) in which, as I understand it, a kind of ecumenical movement emerged across the various 'new social movements', from gay to black, from Marxist to feminist, and so forth. It is, then, that 'federated' left that the film projects in a kind of Utopian vision, setting it against the narrow and provincial patriotism of the Jubilee. And in the present context it is also surely something of that vision of a counter-Europe, a Europe of the federated lumpens and marginals, that is called on to out-trump and cancel the official image of Common Market Europe distributed like travel leaflets from the various chancelleries. This is clearly the most powerful alternate model of federation offered in the various films, and would, if successful, reorient them all around itself. Thus, for example, the Godard 'strange encounter' of the various European social specimens is scarcely activated or sprung into positive motion by the distant echo of Solidarity on its outer fringes, but might be subject to a kind of powerful synthesising and totalising emergence in closer proximity to *Young Soul Rebels*.

The problem with all this is, however, the only too well-known exceptionality of the British situation, which paradoxically has come today to mean the opposite of what it used to betoken, namely the last genuinely radical and politicised zone in the new Europe. I'm willing to stand corrected if I am mistaken in thinking that even on the level of the politics of race, none of the other European 'partners' includes movements of this vitality and national significance. Meanwhile, in contradistinction to the USA, where similar race and gender movements have taken root, but of a ferocious sectarianism and separatism, only the 'left' in Britain seems to offer a common space in which all these movements are willing to be associated and to forge a common political culture. So from all these perspectives Julian's film (unfortunately) marks a uniquely Utopian situation, which may well not find resonance across the checkerboard of the EC. Perhaps in this larger situation some cultural attention to the new mechanisms of transnational power which are being set in place is preferable to a (premature) celebration of an alternate cultural alliance or federation. At any rate I shall be very curious to know the responses of other Europeans to this British vision.

DISCUSSION

Colin MacCabe

I spend much of my time going to conferences which discuss what we should do regarding funding. There is, according to Dieter Koslick, the head of the Hamburg film fund, something like £300 million worth of film subsidy in Western Europe. This is a rough calculation of the subsidies and monies made available by television stations. So there isn't, funnily enough, a shortage of money. What there is, is a shortage of ideas about how that money can be used in film-making which will actually have a cultural impact. If you look at Germany, Westphalia decided about six months ago to put DM45 million (£15 million) into a production fund. But they have no idea about what kind of films they want to make and what kind of audience they are trying to address. So the problem is not money but ideas.

The aim of this conference was to provide a way of thinking about what kind of cinema might be at stake. These are real questions for me and I have been very encouraged by many of the ideas I have heard today, particularly the redefinition of art cinema which John Caughie talked about and some of the things Stuart Hall said, which can be fed, in useful and interesting ways, into the debates that are going on all the time about what to do.

Vladimir Padunov

In 1990 there were more than 300 films made in the Soviet Union, a substantial increase over the number of films produced annually during the years of centralised administrative command control over the film industry. That's not the problem. The problem takes two forms. Firstly, the attempts to reorganise the film industry between 1986 and 1990 were geared at increasing the autonomy of film-makers and improving the quality of films. This turned out to be a wet

91

dream because the only thing it takes to make films in the Soviet Union just now is roubles. And there's nothing one can do with roubles apart from wallpapering one's apartment or making films. This is the reason that films by many contemporary Soviet directors are not funded by the government but by co-operatives.

The second problem is the question of who gets to see those films. In this country you have a greater likelihood of seeing a contemporary Soviet film than a Soviet citizen would. Here, you can see Yuri Mamin's *Sideburns* or Kira Muratova's *Asthenic Syndrome*, which are still unavailable for screening in the Soviet Union. The problem is neither the quality nor the quantity of Soviet films produced, but rather who controls the screening rights and distribution. That question was never posed by the Union of Cinematographers in the attempt to reorganise the Soviet film industry. In part this is because words like 'commercial distribution', 'retailing' and 'wholesaling' don't exist in Russian, partly because those professions have not existed before now. So it's very easy for someone from the black market simply to move in and take control. This does not mean that the value of an American film for a Soviet audience is infinitely higher than that of a film by Alexandr Sokurov, it simply means that Sokurov can get the funds to make a film but has no means to screen it within the Soviet Union.

Question from audience

I want to ask Colin MacCabe what he meant by ideas which make cultural effects?

Colin MacCabe

The question is not, I think, simply of making films; it's making films which actually then become part of the currency of intellectual and political debate within the culture. The problem in Europe is not a shortage in some simple sense of production funds, but rather the fact that it is not European films which become the places around which political, ideological and cultural discussion take place.

Reply from audience

My experience is exactly the opposite: wherever I go I find hundreds of ideas and experiments being made in very small pockets of Britain.

What there isn't is the money or the commitment to allow those ideas to develop. If you look at the history of British cinema in the 70s, those experiments were killed off precisely by the people who have the power to decide what to produce and what not to produce. So I find it extraordinary to hear that suddenly there is all this money and no ideas.

Colin MacCabe

There are two things to be said. One, the money I talked about is in Europe, but there are pathetically small production funds in Britain. Secondly, I would have a very strong disagreement with you about your analysis of the 70s but I don't want to talk too much.

Question from audience

I'd like to address this question to Fredric Jameson. You ended on a rather enigmatic note. What are the strategic implications of what you said?

Fredric Jameson

It isn't for me to deduce strategic implications; but what was at least tactically implicit in my remarks was some advice that included the recommendation of a far greater suspicion of North American culture and power than anything I have heard here. There is a very deep contradiction in the radical and energising effects of the US counter-cultural tradition. I'm sure this has played a positive role in political images such as that offered to us by Isaac Julien. But culture always needs to be converted into politics for its potential to become measurable. If the vitality of American black music is understood to document the vitality of American social life or the exemplary nature of the American political and economic system, then terrible illusions will be fostered that are likely to drain British left politics of its energies. A certain looseness in American social arrangements, a certain failure of the American superego to constitute itself as massively as elsewhere – peculiarities which enable the emergence of rich compensatory alternative cultural movements – should scarcely be celebrated as indices of the benefits of late capitalism, consumerism and North American imperialism (against which those movements are precisely in their various ways so many reactions).

93

As for official Europe itself, a conservative and authoritarian Europe can function progressively if, like Gaullism, it has the will to set limits on US power and omnipotence. The weakness of such a Europe lies, however, in its mass-cultural debility and dependency, and its imports of essentially American cultural products (in film even more than in music). There are also reasons to raise the issue of distribution at this point. Can one conceive of the films we have seen here crossing the former European borders and being enjoyed universally from Brittany to the Oder–Neisse? Or will this constellated Europe not tend commercially to be smothered with a uniformity of American and Hollywood film and television exports, reserving its former high culture, now its counter-culture, to its own national localities, like wines that don't travel and recipes that neighbours don't like? Any materialist examination of the new Europe culture ought presumably to begin with just such matters of distribution, financing, local production and the like.

Comment from audience

I think this conference has suggested very forcefully how useful it would be to look at film as a form of hybrid. The other two areas, which have come over more weakly, although they are there in the European tradition, are those of the 'art film' and realism. But I also think that to recognise the tradition comprising these three issues, one would have to have a far less negative view of the concept of Europe than that suggested by Fredric Jameson.

Patrizia Lombardo

I'm a sort of Utopian so I never have a negative vision when I think in creative terms and in terms of technique inside the film. I really don't know much about the question of money. What I do think is that all the films which were chosen for this conference generate a debate about what is Europe and what we can do with it. I'm glad that the new generation of film-makers does not deal with the notion of pure realism nor with the notion of the art film, but rather a kind of product which comes from the interrelation of film and television. And in that sense, although I'm a big fan of film, I have no nostalgia. This is the age of television. It seems ridiculous to want to destroy it, to adopt what I call the 'Amish position' – 'we are in the country, we don't dress the same, we don't use cars'. These are, after all, the 90s. So in that sense I'm glad that we don't talk any more about art films and realism but rather that we talk about this hybrid which is something between the old idea of cinema and the input of television, for better or worse.

Question from audience

I want to ask a question which hasn't come up. It's about European co-production, a trend of co-operation between different nationalities and different sources of funding which has been accelerating as we approach 1992. Does the panel consider that this will vitiate or destroy the national tradition of film-making (if there is such a thing), or do they think that it's the key to the future and to a unification of European film-making?

Nancy Condee

One of the things which has struck me throughout this conference is the ambivalent relationship to hybridity as a whole. I bring this up because I think Americans in particular have a completely different relationship to the idea of hybridity. We warm ourselves with the notion of the melting pot, which is a way of both allowing diversity and erasing difference among various peoples. If there are any European imperialists out there, what you need is a good metaphor like the melting pot. The identity crisis mentioned at the outset of this conference by Godard as characteristic of American consciousness is not at all characteristic: we're not involved in an identity crisis; we know exactly who we are as a culture. We simply don't recognise that there are any *other* cultures out there. We invade other people, not to resolve our identity but to sell violent, white, male American culture to the rest of the world. What we see in European culture is an ambivalence about your own hybridity, because you don't have a good explanatory myth like the melting pot to make sense of it for you.

Colin MacCabe

I'm just going to make one final comment in relation to that. *Young Soul Rebels* is a gay movie, a black movie, but most importantly for me, it's a European hybrid. If you look at its production credits, it was funded from Spain, France, Germany and England, and yet is a film which is able to reflect a very specific and local set of concerns. And therefore I think there is everything to fight for, and the next two or three years hold out a great deal of optimism. I hope this conference has contributed to it.

APPENDIX 1
Jean-Luc Godard in Conversation with Colin MacCabe

Colin MacCabe

Jean-Luc, I'd like to start with *Passion* and ask you how far would you think of that film in relation to the problem of how to put together the popular form of the cinema with the traditional culture of Europe? Does that in any way relate to what you thought you were doing when you made the film?

Jean-Luc Godard

I don't think so, but then I don't understand at all these things about Europe. I maybe feel European – I'm from two countries, French Switzerland and France – and because of that I've seen the difficulties of *frontière*, of borderlines. But I don't believe at all that you will be free to come to any country without showing your passport. Today as a Swiss citizen, I'm considered by the British authorities as different from citizens of EC countries. Europe was created by Charlemagne and it took us twelve hundred years to come back to the boundaries drawn by the Aix-la-Chapelle Treaty. Is it going forward or is it going backward? I don't know. But getting back to *Passion*, no, I didn't think of it in the way you suggested.

Colin MacCabe

But in *Passion* you have the great tradition of European painting.

Jean-Luc Godard

I was interested in paintings as I am interested in novels. I consider Wilhelm Meister as one of my cousins, Ivan Karamazov as one of my uncles. Those people are my family.

Most of the talking about Europe today is mainly done by people living in Brussels, but Brussels has no painting, no literature. Greece is considered part of Europe, not because of Pericles and Plato but because it's part of NATO.

If I refer to my knowledge of movies, pictures, or the idea of movie-making, was strongly linked to the identity of a nation. That's why there is no French television, or Italian, or British, or American television. There can be only one television because it's not related to nation. It's related to finance or commerce. Movie-making at the beginning was related to the identity of the nation and there have been very few 'national' cinemas. In my opinion there is no Swedish cinema but there are Swedish movie-makers – some very good ones, such as Stiller and Bergman. There have been only a handful of cinemas: Italian, German, American and Russian. This is because when countries were inventing and using motion pictures, they needed an image of themselves. The Russian cinema arrived at a time they needed a new image. And in the case of Germany, they had lost a war and were completely corrupted and needed a new idea of Germany. At the time the new Italian cinema emerged, Italy was completely lost – it was the only country which fought with the Germans, then against the Germans. They strongly needed to see a new reality and this was provided by neo-realism. Today, if you put all these people in one so-called 'Eurocountry', you have nothing; since television is television, you only have America.

Colin MacCabe

The next thing is the *nouvelle vague* in which another generation finds an identity, but an identity which doesn't reject America but rather reworks those American images.

Jean-Luc Godard

At the beginning we were strongly against the French cinema as it was then. We defended a lot of individual American movie-makers and said 'they are the real artists' – we said Hitchcock can be the author of his films as well as Proust. It was perhaps an exaggeration, but after that his name came above the title of the film whereas before it was under.

We were defending the old Chaplin and the young Cassavettes as well, against some Hollywood way of producing films. I was not against Hollywood but I was against the fact the Hollywood was like the Roman Empire. I'm not against Julius Caesar – if he keeps in Rome. As you know, he came to Switzerland. The Swiss people hated their country from the beginning and wanted to go to 'Le midi de la France', but Julius Caesar didn't want this and forced them to remain where they were, and that's what makes Switzerland today!

Colin MacCabe

There is a change in your work from the influence of 50s and 60s American cinema. In the 80s you look at the great paintings and the great texts – *King Lear* – and the great Christian tradition.

Jean-Luc Godard

I've gone back to my past. It's well known that when you become older you go back to your childhood, you are beginning to understand your inheritance. I was raised by a rich, tolerant and educated family. I was not taught that Lenin was a great revolutionary but I was taught that Goethe was a great writer.

But I don't understand the obsession with this thing called Europe. Today, culture is American; it has been accepted by the audience all over the world. There was only one country and political regime which tried to fight America in this context and that was Nazi Germany and UFA studios. For six or seven years German movie-making dominated Europe. The coming of sound was also a fight between America and Germany. But the Germans were the one country which tried to make the Europeans feel as Jacques Delors wants today, with the people united!

Colin MacCabe

In your earlier cinema in relation to Mozambique there is a great interest in the whole problem of how the Third World would find ways to make images of themselves. This concern seems to have gone from your work.

Jean-Luc Godard

I was still Utopian at the time, and I don't believe now it can be made on an individual level. The imperialism of television has meant that cinema has to be supported. Movies are not making money in theatres, only in festivals or on TV screens. People prefer to see a little image than a projection. A projection is like looking at the sky, but watching television is not. It doesn't reveal reality, it shows our fear of seeing real life. TV is not showing that every day forty thousand children are dying in the world. But movie-making is still capable of working on such a level.

Colin MacCabe

So what you are saying is that effectively what we have is a global culture which is American?

Jean-Luc Godard

No, no. We have a global culture which is not American but which is becoming American. The problem is that Europe has no style. Look at cars today. The Japanese are making better German cars than the Germans.

Colin MacCabe

At first I thought you were saying that America just rules. Now you seem to be saying that we must find ways in which it is possible to have a wider variety or diversity of culture.

Jean-Luc Godard

But we have it. The difficulty is trying to keep it. I've a strong feeling that personally, as a movie-maker, I should be able to turn out better movies today than five or ten years ago. But I'm actually less capable. On every movie I've made I have a feeling that 'Oh, I see now,' but by then the movie is over. What I've shot should be the script and the real movie should have been the equivalent of what Stroheim or Griffith or Murnau was doing. When we started making movies it was a beginning for us, but it was also an end of an artistic movement which had

100

been a European movement. Movie-making had been invented by Europeans, mainly Germans.

Today, 99 per cent of movie-making is done by white boys from industrial countries. The Chinese didn't invent it, they have another tradition and philosophy. The Indians didn't invent it. It was only done by white boys in industrial countries, even if today there are some white women also making movies. I feel guilty about it. I was raised only in European culture, I didn't know about the Chinese and the Indians. That is why I always try with my movies to go to an unknown country – even if that country is my neighbour. As Kafka said, as I referred to in *New Wave*, 'The positive is given to us. We have to make the negative ourselves.' And film stock is not by chance called a negative.

Question from audience

Referring to what you said about cinemas in relation to national identity, if neo-realism was a moment when the Italians needed their identity, what is the moment for French cinema?

Jean-Luc Godard

I think there is no French cinema, but there have been French film-makers and the French are so good at talking about themselves that everybody thought there was a French cinema. There have been four cinemas which have shown reality in a new way through a new form: a Russian cinema, a German cinema, an Italian cinema and an American cinema. The Americans imposed their way of movie-making all over the world and are now doing it with TV. They invented the industrial way of movie-making which brought an artistic way of movie-making because of some strong individuals. Most of them, in the beginning, were European.

Today we are making American movies with Japanese equipment. This obliges you to make this sort of movie rather than that sort of movie. It's not innocent. And even in France, which has tried to protect its cinema in good ways, there is a loss of identity – they are speaking English. Why should this be? I don't understand. Who decides what people want to see? I would prefer for a time, instead of seeing ten American movies, to see one bad Turkish movie, one bad Belgian movie, one bad African movie and so on. This would be Europe.

Colin MacCabe

But you then come dangerously close to some of the initiatives from Brussels which are designed exactly to enable you to see bad European movies.

Question from audience

Do you think English-speaking nations are more prone to becoming Americanised than France, for example?

Jean-Luc Godard

Yes, because for a very long time they have been linked to America because of the similarity of the language. And there is no longer a British film industry today. I think that the British were never very gifted movie-makers, although I do have a lot of admiration for a movie produced by Colin – *Distant Voices, Still Lives*. But because the identity of the British was formed a long time ago by people like Gladstone and Nelson, they have an image of themselves and they don't seem to need another.

Colin MacCabe

I would agree with you that the British didn't need cinema because there was that image which was fixed. It's in Shakespeare. It's no accident that they made *Henry V* and called it a great European movie. But that image has nothing to do with Britain now. So perhaps we do need movies to give us another image of ourselves.

Jean-Luc Godard

Yes, but maybe it doesn't go through movies any more because it's so corrupted. Television is not producing images. It is making pro-grammes which do nothing. Television shows us something like the Gulf War. It will tell us that, for example, the number of American casualties was 388. At the same time the number of casualties from crime in America was 387 – you won't find these images on television, only in some good newspapers. It wasn't West Germany who pulled

102

down the Berlin wall but rather the people from the east. We could at least thank them.

Colin MacCabe

But there was an American film shown at Cannes this year called *Boyz N' the Hood*, which is about ordinary American life in which young kids in Los Angeles kill each other all the time.

Comment from audience

If you look at identities in Europe now, they don't relate to the traditional concepts of European identity.

Jean-Luc Godard

We have in Europe more or less lost our identity, mainly through an acceptance of American culture. For me, painting and movie-making is not culture. A novel is not culture – it's art. Mozart is not culture, but distributing Mozart on RCA compact disc is culture. This is very different. But I don't think the cure for this lost identity is to try to construct a bigger identity and call it 'European'. The Russians have tried, the Nazis have tried, even Thatcher tried here.

Colin MacCabe

I'm not unhappy about having lost some of our identity. These European identities, the kind of English identity that Shakespeare produces, it's a pretty nasty one. And the notion that losing that is a bad thing doesn't seem to be the case to me at all. It seems therefore that the question about how you get identities in Europe can be a very positive one.

Jean-Luc Godard

Half of Yugoslavia wants to split into ten. Why not? They should agree rather than fighting – but they don't agree. An image is something different. It was linked in the beginning with identity. Today it's not that, it is a way to see things the same way, which doesn't reveal the truth.

Movie-making is difficult. I always try to make young movie-makers aware of how difficult it is to make a good movie. I ask them to think of their own day as a story. If you make this the Hollywood way, or the BBC way, you talk in clichés and you know very well that this is not your real day. Because of TV we think today that it is easy to make an image. It's not, it's the most difficult thing. I was always amazed by the fact that movie-makers sometimes don't make more than one film in three years. A painter like Rembrandt was seeing his brushes every ten seconds. Spielberg is not seeing his camera more than once every three years — how can be use it? A surgeon can't do that, a taxi driver can't do it, so what makes a movie-maker different today?

Questions from audience

I recently saw *Hail Mary* and was so surprised at how different the style is from other films. How did you get a crew to work in this way?

Jean-Luc Godard

I always have difficulty with the crew, and I've tried to make it as small as possible. When I say very small I mean about two or three people — a very small crew for an average American film is about eighty people. I like to work with new people and I prefer to use a local cinematographer. To work as a painter or a novelist is a solitary job, but to be a film-maker you have to work with other people. My main partner in movie-making is the producer, so the creation is coming more from the link between art and money than from the technical side of things. I'm not very good at working with technicians — this is a weakness in my movie-making.

Questions from audience

You said at one point that there had been a German cinema, a Russian cinema, an American cinema and an Italian cinema. Is there now *only* American cinema?

Jean-Luc Godard

Yes. But it's no more a cinema. The problem with America is that they have a big problem with identity. In the last movie I made I used a quote from an old novel which said something very interesting about America. It said that America is only fighting a civil war: when they were English they fought the English, when they became American they fought between themselves. When they became civilised by Germans and acquired German culture, then they dropped bombs on Germany. America only makes war with countries which have the same faults as themselves. You see that with Iraq. Iraq has exactly the same faults as America, they don't know who they are. They have no identity. And when you have no identity you are searching for an image.

Question from audience

What is your greatest ambition?

Jean-Luc Godard

To be less tired.

APPENDIX 2
Mapping the European Mind

Antoine Compagnon

The spirit of Europe, or the European mind, has become quite a fashionable topic lately. What is it? Does such a thing even exist, or is it a fiction, like one of those ideal objects Russell was trying to get rid of in philosophy – the present king of France, or the president of Great Britain – descriptions that denote nothing, and which therefore render any proposition that includes them false. What about the European mind? It seems to be present everywhere and yet invisible.

In 1993, the open unified market will be an irrefutable and incontrovertible reality. I teach in the United States, where people feel quite uneasy about that prospect, which will turn Europe into the largest consumers' market in the world. In France, when I returned in the summer of 1988, after the presidential elections and a campaign which had given rise to much discussion about Europe, it was easy to notice that everyone had suddenly become painfully aware of the 1993 deadline. We are all worried by the implications of the single market for our jobs and daily lives. Every profession is hastening to become more competitive, to modernise and rationalise: banks, insurance, as well as all the culture industry. One implication of this obvious and deep anxiety is that Europe, which has until now been consistently boring, seems to arouse passion. Europe had to do with agriculture, quotas, demonstrations in Brussels. Whenever the evening news in France came to a European topic, people would turn their TVs off. That was before zapping. What a bore! And how arcane! Now, and this is striking, Europe is a very concrete project, perhaps even too concrete, and will soon become a blunt reality. Monsieur Giscard d'Estaing said during the campaign for the European elections of 1989 that there was one chance out of three that Europe would fail in the next few years. You would not launch a rocket under such odds.

Let us assume Europe will exist in 1993. But what is it in our heads, our French, Greek, British heads? If the nation-states that originated during the Renaissance and reached their climax during the nineteenth century undoubtedly remain the fundamental reality, politically, historically, as well as culturally, what could we call 'Europeanity', or 'Europeanness'? I am sorry for the neologisms, which are meant to convey an idea of Europe, or some sort of European identity, common for instance to the countries which signed the Helsinki agreements in 1975, at the Conference on Security and Co-operation in Europe, which is as close as one can get to a political definition of Europe. The conference included the members of NATO and the Warsaw Pact, neutral countries like Sweden and Austria, and even Switzerland, some miniature states like the Vatican, San Marino, Lichtenstein, as well as the Mediterranean islands of Cyprus and Malta. Only Albania and Andorra, it seems, were missing. Now, what could they have in common apart from the certitude that Europe would be the first region of the world to be obliterated in case of a nuclear war? This paper was prepared before the upheavals in Eastern Europe during the summer and fall of 1989, which might render the idea of the single market obsolete even before it is implemented. In any case, if no idea of Europe does exist, it is urgent to invent one, so that Europe, whatever it becomes, will not find itself against culture. You will note: (1) that my perspective is not limited to the Common Market, and (2) that, albeit sceptical, my standpoint on Europeanness is not nostalgic.

Pierre Larousse, the founder of the publishing house, and the author of the well-known *Dictionary of the Nineteenth Century*, wrote under the entry Europe: 'Europe is something only as long as it is called France, England, Russia, Austria, Prussia, Spain, etc. Here the particular prevails over the general. It could not be the same with America, Asia, Africa, the South Sea Islands; there, the general prevails over the particular.' One will certainly be quick to react against Larousse, this enlightened Republican who wrote under the entry on Bonaparte in his dictionary: 'born on Ajaccio in 1769, died in Saint-Cloud, near Paris, on the 18th of Brumaire, year VIII of the French Republic, one and indivisible.' But his definition of Europe would be typical of the ethnocentrism and Europeocentrism that served as the necessary ideological basis for the colonisation of those other continents devoid of particularities. What is this generality that reigns outside Europe but a *tabula rasa* waiting for civilisation? That is not, however, the point I want to make, and the *New York Times* correspondent, Flora Lewis, in her recent book, *Europe: A Tapestry of Nations*, still sways between the two paths outlined by Larousse: 'I have tried to show', she says, 'that there is such a place as Europe, such a thing as European, even though the moment you approach to look more closely it breaks up into kaleidoscopic fragments.' She has spent many years in Europe, but her view should remain that of an outsider, and there is no doubt that for an outsider such a thing as a European unity, generality, or identity exists beyond the complexity of the cultures and the picturesque of the landscapes. Before the Second World War, Greeks travelling to Paris or Berlin said that they were going to Europe. And now of course Greece is paradoxically a member of the Common Market. The Jews of Morocco or Tunisia also used the phrase 'going to Europe' when they left North Africa. And what about the trip through Europe any self-respecting American college kid will feel bound to take: London, Paris, Rome, Madrid in ten days? Will he get a sense of unity or complexity? Seen from abroad, from America, Asia, Africa, Australia, without its particularities being lost, Europe exists. As a matter of fact, it is most often in the 'Travel' section of the *New York Times* that Europe is mentioned, and seldom in the main one. But, and this is why I cited Larousse's standpoints on Europe and Napoleon, Europe is not a continent but a peninsula, the western tip of Eurasia and an archipelago of diversities, where all imperial dreams historically failed. What can the culture of an archipelago be like? Europeans do not believe in Europe, but those who do not have it miss it and long for it – I hardly exaggerate. This sounds like the conventional definition of the object of desire that nobody ever possesses.

Europe, as I said, is that part of the world that would most likely disappear first in the event of a nuclear war. What would then be obliterated? Only particularities? Or a civilisation? A culture, in the German or English sense of a set of values, rituals, observances pertaining to a distinctive social community? What I called a spirit, a *Geist*, that is, a Europe of non-identity, altogether international and local, as opposed to a Europe of nationalities. The spirit of Europe as such, in the sense of a consciousness, cannot in any case be of long standing, but its late advent should not mask the simultaneity of an important number of major movements, in the political, economic, religious, and intellectual orders, the European dimension of which is beyond all question. The French essayist Julien Benda, in his *Discourse to the European Nation* of 1933, mentioned the crusades and the revolutions, the colonisations, the Reformation, the advent of class struggle. But, as Benda concluded, 'all these European movements did strictly nothing for the unity of Europe. Why? Because Europe, in achieving them, was not aware of them as European; because the people of Europe were subject to the community of their interests, lived the identity of their feelings, but did not perceive them as such.' It is in part this failure to recognise the Europeanness of our past that ought to be overcome in order to appreciate what is the present state of the European consciousness and what future it can lay claim to.

My attempt at defining Europeanness is not antiquarian or archaeological. But I would like to be historical, as I feel the need to rethink past and present phenomena in the terms of their European coinci-

108

dence. It is also necessary to catch up with the most recent movements, in art and society. There is, however, an obvious trap one should avoid falling into: the danger that the mapping out of the idea of Europe will turn into an apology, in fact erecting its tombstone and burying it under the commonplaces of humanism. Is the European idea liberty, democracy, literacy, style? Europe invented the individual; it also invented the death of the individual. Europe invented humanism; it also invented crimes against humanity. We should not forget the vicious and nasty Europe that has been frozen by forty years of Cold War. But there is no reason either to take the blame for everything that went wrong. The European idea should lead to a survey of its problematical *topoi*, *loci*, or places, its conflicting, controversial, paradoxical haunts. Mapping out the spirit of Europe is also and by necessity doubting it.

In the following remarks, I will offer a brief survey of the *loci* of Europeanness. As with all classification, it has some arbitrariness, but it tries to invent objects that cross nationalities, and their conflicts and exchanges. Far from pulling out of the encyclopedia what could be labelled European, or praising a defunct Europe – the one, as I said, of liberty, progress, toleration, those belated icons – the challenge lies in conceiving some exemplary places of European consciousness in the 1990s, places that are grounded historically and have a modern or post-modern aura.

It seems to me – and I rely here on the work I have done with Jacques Seebacher for the preparation of a volume on European culture – that they can be searched for in three main fields, which I will briefly outline. (1) The major references, the historical and geographical landmarks that stand out in the present representation that Europeans have of Europe. In a word, the emblems which constitute the time and space of the Europeans. (2) The few concepts that contribute to a European mentality, be it political, economic, religious, social, etc. That is, the notions which describe the mind of Europe. (3) The aesthetic values that govern European taste. That is, the tastes that have shaped a European style in the arts. Of course, in all the above, there is some confusion between what is European culture and what pertains to Western civilisation at large. It also seems crucial to distinguish between what is European by its origins, and what can be presently called European. With all these implicit criticisms in mind, let me none the less proceed and give some examples of how a topic of Europe could be sketched.

With regard to the direction I mentioned first, that of the European representation of time and space, the aim would be to achieve neither a chronology nor an atlas, but a mapping out of major symbolic landmarks. Proceeding with a survey of the ten most important dates in that perspective, one would come up with a list. Without producing the distinctive entries, one could simply say that it would include definitions of borders between Europe and the East, like 1683, when the Turks were in Vienna, failures of empires, like 843, the treaty of Verdun and the partition of the Carolingian Empire, and diasporas. Those dates would deal with the relations of Europe with its neighbours, its borders, its invaders, as well as events whose supranational repercussion is undeniable. From the viewpoint of geography, the equivalent of those events would be axes of communication, for instance, rivers such as the Rhine, Volga, or Danube, to which the Italian writer Claudio Magris has recently dedicated a volume. Or the Channel, or the line Leipzig–Dresden–Cracow–Kiev, or the North/South and East/West polarities, present in each nation and which are reproduced at the scale of Europe itself. But a spatiotemporal topic should be undermined and include an imaginary dimension: it is clear that Elsinore, for instance, belongs to the European landmarks.

In connection with the European mentality, many recent and valuable historical works – influenced more or less by the Annales school founded by Marc Bloch and Lucien Febvre – like the *History of Private Life*, or the *History of the City*, give us an idea of where to look for a transnational culture. Three orders ought to be taken into consideration, those of the sacred, the civic, and the domestic. The vision that Europe has of its others, and that which the others have of Europe, should be explored. In short, what needs to be done is some sort of anthropology of Europe. Let me just evoke some of those categories of myths that pertain to the European mentality. And why not begin with the body? To put it simply, is there a European body, past and present? Nudity, shame, chastity: what is the range of these taboos and values? Or the individual, already mentioned. Europe, as I said, both invented and abolished it. The individual, as conceived in terms of natural law, is but a moment in Western rationality and is now threatened by genetic engineering. Or otherness, which certainly is one of the crucial categories of the European mind. The Renaissance conception of otherness, in Montaigne and Shakespeare, precedes and prepares the formation of a modern Western consciousness, and already it is from the start filled with ambivalence. Montaigne, who opens himself to the other, is considered a forefather of modern ethnology before Rousseau, but he uses the other to deliver a lesson to his fellow Europeans.

Acknowledging and denying otherness belong to one and the same gesture, which I would tend to judge profoundly European. More generally, each category deemed to be European contains or implies its own negation: like progress, or humanism, or universality. At the root of those negations, doubt, it seems to me, might be the essential

110

European faculty: not only Descartes's hyperbolic doubt, that is, the strength to make a *tabula rasa* of one's own reason, as has been achieved repeatedly in the history of Western thought and science, but also the doubt which I would call, with Hegel, the moment of 'unhappy consciousness'. We have most often retained from Hegel's *Philosophy of Mind* the concept of *Aufhebung*, or sublation, which is the glorification of linear progress and causal history. Few thinkers have insisted, like Nietzsche, on the unending and unbound negation to be found in Hegel, on consciousness as the 'consciousness of its own contradiction', on, so to speak, consciousness as the 'crisis of European consciousness'. As Georges Bataille put it: 'Scandal is the same thing as consciousness: a consciousness without scandal is alienated consciousness – a consciousness, as experience proves, of clear and distinct objects, intelligible, or thought to be so.' I see this acting out of doubt, for instance, in the particular form of European masochism or guilt which is the other side of colonialism and which now leads us to take the blame for everything that went wrong in the world, and to ignore or deny that colonialism was not only destructive. Baudelaire's *Héautontimotouménos*, or self-tormentor, after Terentius and Swinburne, is a great European figure, alongside Hamlet, Don Quixote, Faust: torturing the other, he tortures himself as well. I see also this doubt in melancholy, spleen, *ennui*, present in all our cultures as the black angel of faith. But to conclude with the European mind on a less sombre note, I should mention civility, or courtliness. Here, I am speaking as a European who has been living for some time overseas, even though in New York, which is in many ways a European outpost somewhere between London or Paris and the Far West, though spiritually much closer to London and Paris. But even in New York, the lack of a courtly tradition is a major element of difference. As a matter of fact, those elements of the European mind that undermine the European mind – doubt, unhappy consciousness, nihilism, melancholy, etc. – can certainly not be found to the same extent in what could be called colonial or transplanted Europe, that is, places like North America, Australia, South Africa, Israel. I offer this as a hypothesis, and I do not mean that some more uncertainty would not be welcome here and there. Now, with courtly manners I feel more confident, as I have seen so many of my American friends radically baffled and put off by a conversation in the Old World, a ritual where one does not care as much about the topic as the talking itself. As Montaigne, a perfect *cortegiano* and *honnête homme*, put it, those who think that the pleasure of hunting is in the catch have understood nothing. With courtly life, it is snobbism, distinction, *decorum, sprezzatura* or *désinvolture*, which the English 'ease' renders insufficiently, like an unselfconsicous self-consciousness, the oxymoron incarnate, or

111

the supreme dandy, it is all those terms which hardly makes sense outside Europe.

Moving to the third and last area I mentioned above, Europe's aesthetic identity, I can describe it of course in a very conventional way: as comparative literature has traditionally been understood, that is, the study of cross-cultural influences or the analysis of Western myths. Thus numerous monographies have been devoted to the dissemination of the Gothic or the Enlightenment in Northern or Eastern Europe. I see here two possible escape routes: one would insist on theory, the other on reception. Let me limit the arguments to a few examples. By theory, I mean rhetoric, and I do not restrict it to the Great Age of Eloquence. Many figures of a specifically European rhetoric could be evoked, but I shall mention only two which seem central: allegory and blasphemy. Allegory first: when the American critic Paul de Man argued a while ago that allegory was the central trope and topos of literature, he revived an ancient tradition, Greek as well as Judaic and Christian, best encapsulated in Saint Paul's 'The letter killeth, but the spirit giveth life.' Through allegory, we understand figurative sense, plurality of meaning, the essence itself of literature and art. One should add that allegory is the most general model of access to fiction as such. At its side stands blasphemy. It is the Salman Rushdie affair that made me see it as the guardian angel of allegory, I mean its double, its inseparable companion. In fact, allegory makes blasphemy acceptable. Blasphemy, transgression, satire and parody: from Boccaccio and Rabelais to Proust and Joyce, and probably to rock'n roll, it is the sacred fount of European art.

The second escape route would be reception, that is a history of taste. Here, across the Channel, the best example I can give is Francis Haskell's *Rediscoveries in Art*, a study of the redistribution and revaluation of the major art collections at the end of the eighteenth century, during the French Revolution, the Napoleonic wars. The paintings of the Duke of Orleans, for instance, were sold in London and went to Berlin and Saint Petersburg. Italian and Spanish paintings enriched the Louvre. Haskell argues that this fascinating movement was not favourable to the modern. It remains, however, one of the major aesthetic upheavals of European history, and the prelude to the international art market of capitalism. Other examples could be cited in the nineteenth and twentieth centuries, or when the art market became international before the First World War, with cubism and abstraction, or, not to limit myself to a Europe of high culture, when the image was industrialised after the Second World War, or when the music market became global and ignored linguistic barriers. But I shall end here, insisting once again that though conscious of history – history, which I have not mentioned as perhaps the most perverse European invention

112

– my overview is not historical. Europe is present everywhere and yet invisible; the circumference is everywhere and the centre nowhere. We should be wary of a definition that makes it akin to God. That is why I have tried to map out the idea of Europe in such a pedestrian fashion.

This essay originally appeared in *Critical Quarterly*, vol. 32, no. 2, Summer 1990.

APPENDIX 3
Credits and Synopses of Films

(These are selected credits and synopses from the Monthly Film Bulletin, published by the BFI. For a full list of credits, synopsis and critical essay on each film, see the relevant issue of MFB.)

THE TEMPEST

United Kingdom 1979   Director: Derek Jarman

Distributor: Mainline; Production Company: Boyd's Company; Executive Producer: Don Boyd; Producers: Guy Ford, Mordecai Schreiber; Screenplay: Derek Jarman, based on the play by William Shakespeare; Photography: Peter Middleton; Editors: Lesley Walker, Annette D'Alton; Production Designer: Yolanda Sonnabend.

Cast
Prospero: Heathcote Williams; Ariel: Karl Johnson; Miranda: Toyah Wilcox; Alonso: Peter Bull; Antonio: Richard Warwick; Goddess: Elizabeth Welch; Caliban: Jack Birkett; Gonzalo: Ken Campbell; Ferdinand: David Meyer; Sebastian: Neil Cunningham; Stephano: Christopher Biggins; Sycorax: Claire Davenport.

Synopsis
Prospero, the deposed Duke of Milan, lives and practises his magic on an enchanted island with his daughter Miranda, his monstrous servant, Caliban, and an enslaved spirit, Ariel. Discovering that his enemies – his brother, Antonio, the King of Naples, Alonso, and Alonso's brother Sebastian – are sailing close by the island, Prospero conjures up a storm. The entire ship's company are subsequently cast ashore and into Prospero's power. Accompanying his enemies are his erstwhile faithful courtier, Gonzalo, Alonso's son Ferdinand, and a pair of drunken fools, Stephano and Trinculo. In two straggling

114

groups, they are lured towards Prospero's castle by the bewitching power of Ariel's song. Separated from the rest, Ferdinand meets and falls in love with Miranda, but is reduced to miserable bondage by Prospero, who intends to test his devotion. While Alonso searches for his son, Sebastian and Antonio plot to murder him and usurp his throne. Ariel, however, has them all under his master's spell, and while Caliban teams up with Stephano and Trinculo (in a parallel plot to overthrow his master), Prospero's magic works to disarm his enemies and to halt them in their tracks until he is ready to deal with them. Prospero finally countenances the betrothal of Ferdinand and Miranda, admonishes the fools' plot, and lectures yet forgives his old enemies. Everyone is reconciled in a celebration dance, Prospero fulfils his bargain to free Ariel and, as he leaves the island for good, renounces his magical arts. (MFB, April 1980)

PASSION

France/Switzerland 1982   Director: Jean-Luc Godard

Distributor: Artificial Eye; Production Company: Sara Films/Sonimage/Films A 2 (Paris)/Film et Vidéo Productions (Lausanne)/SSR (Geneva); Producer: Alain Sarde; Screenplay: Jean-Luc Godard; Photography: Raoul Coutard; Editor: Jean-Luc Godard; Art Directors: Serge Marzolff, Jean Bauer; Musical extracts from works by Mozart, Dvořák, Beethoven, Fauré, Ravel.

Cast
Isabelle: Isabelle Huppert; Hana: Hanna Schygulla; Jerzy: Jerzy Radziwilowicz; Michel Gulla: Michel Piccoli; Lazlo: Lazlo Szabo.

Synopsis
Jerzy, a Polish director making a film in France entitled *Passion*, is beset with a variety of difficulties. Not only are his backers concerned about what they perceive as a lack of any real narrative in the film, but he is unable to obtain exactly the lighting he wants for the series of art-history tableaux which are apparently crucial to his theme. These tableaux include pastiches of Goya's *The Sunshade*, *The Naked Maja*, *The Executions of May 3rd, 1808* and *The Family of Charles IV*, Delacroix's *The Entry of the Crusaders into Constantinople* and *Jacob Wrestling with the Angel*, El Greco's *The Assumption of the Virgin*, and Ingres's *The Small Bather*. With members of his film crew, he is lodged in a nearby motel owned by Hanna, the German-born wife of Michel, who manages the local factory. When Michel decides to

dismiss Isabelle, a young woman whom he regards as a trouble-maker, she attempts to involve Jerzy in her situation, but he is too busy persuading Hanna to play a role in *Passion*. Hanna, however, berates her husband for having refused to pay Isabelle compensation for the loss of her job; and a number of employees propose locking Michel out of his own factory. Concurrently, Lazlo, the film's executive producer, informs Jerzy that MGM has agreed to take over the production and offers him a plane ticket for Hollywood. Jerzy, who has become emotionally involved with Hanna, declines the offer and later sleeps with Isabelle. As the shoot comes to a halt, Hanna and Isabelle meet up and, almost on a whim, set off for Poland. Jerzy, too, decides that the time has come for him to return to his homeland. (MFB, June 1983)

WOMEN ON THE VERGE OF A NERVOUS BREAKDOWN

Spain 1988   Director: Pedro Almodóvar

Distributor: Rank; Production Company: El Deseo/Lauren Film, for Orion; Executive Producer: Agustín Almodóvar; Associate Producer: Antonio Lloréns; Screenplay: Pedro Almodóvar; Photography: José Luis Alcaine; Editor: José Salcedo; Set Decorator: Félix Murcia; Music: Bernardo Bonezzi.

Cast
Pepa: Carmen Maura; Carlos: Antonio Banderas; Lucia: Julieto Serrano; Candela: María Barranco; Marisa: Rossy de Palma; Taxi Driver: Guillermo Montesinos; Paulina: Kiti Manver; Christina: Loles Leon; Ivan: Fernando Guillen; Policeman: Angel de Andrés López; 2nd Policeman: José Antonio Navarro.

Synopsis
Madrid. Pepa awakes from a drug-induced sleep to find that her long-term lover Ivan has gone, leaving only an answer-machine message asking her to pack his bags. Pepa, who has just learned that she is pregnant, becomes near-hysterical while she waits for Ivan to call again, and then impulsively puts her penthouse up for rent. By a series of accidents, she finds herself on the trail of Ivan's insane ex-wife Lucia, and discovers that Ivan has a twenty-year-old son Carlos. Back at the apartment Ivan has left another message, and so has Pepa's desperate friend Candela. Early the next day, Candela arrives and claims that she is on the run from the police because of her relationship with a Shi'ite terrorist; co-incidentally, Carlos and his bored

116

girlfriend Marisa arrive with a view to rent the penthouse (which Pepa has partly destroyed in her anguish). When Pepa reveals her connection with Ivan, Carlos agrees to wait for Ivan's call while she goes in search of a good lawyer for Candela. Meanwhile, Marisa falls victim to some tranquilliser-laden *gazpacho* prepared by Pepa for Ivan, and Candela calls the police with a warning that the Shi'ites plan to bomb that evening's flight to Stockholm. Downtown, Pepa has a furious row with the unsympathetic feminist lawyer Paulina de Moralis; she arrives back at the apartment moments ahead of Lucia and two detectives investigating the terrorist tip-off. As Carlos serves the spiked *gazpacho* to an expanding number of visitors, Pepa deduces that Ivan is leaving with his new mistress Paulina on the doomed Stockholm flight. Pepa and Lucia race each other to the airport, where Pepa saves Ivan from Lucia's attempt to shoot him. Remorseful, Ivan suggests that maybe they should get back together, but Pepa realises that now she has no desire to see or even speak to him. (MFB, June 1989)

CHOCOLAT

France 1988   Director: Claire Denis

Distributor: Electric Pictures; Production Company: Cinémanuel/MK2 Productions/Cerito Films/SEPT/Caroline Productions/TFI Films (in co-operation with FODIC, Wim Wenders Production; with the participation of the Centre National de la Cinématographie, SOFICA SOFIMA; in collaboration with WDR); Executive Producers: Alain Belmondo, Gérard Crosnier; Associate Producers: Samuel Mabon, Pierre Llouga Mabout; Screenplay: Claire Denis, Jean-Pol Fargeau; Photography: Robert Alazraki; Editors: Claudine Merlin, Monica Coleman, Sylvie Quester, Marie-Claire Quin; Art Director: Thierry Flamand; Music: Abdullah Ibrahim.

Cast
Protée: Isaach de Bankolé; Aimée: Giúlia Boschi; Young France: Cecile Ducasse; Marc: François Cluzet; Luc: Jean-Claude Adelin; France: Mireille Perrier; Mungo Park: Emmet Judson Williamson; Boothby: Kenneth Cranham; Machinard: Laurent Arnal; Prosper: Jean Bediebe; Courbassol: Jean-Quentin Chatelain.

Synopsis
France, whose father was a *commissaire* in the French colonial administration, visits the remote region of the Cameroons where she spent much of her childhood. She hitches a lift to the airport to catch a plane

117

into the bush from Mungo Park, a black American who has settled in the country. Her mind flashes back to scenes of her youth: she remembers her friendship with the black servant Protée; the Englishman, Boothby, arriving for dinner when her father was away and her mother hastily unpacking her evening dress from a trunk; the upheaval caused when a plane crashed nearby and the house was invaded by the crew and passengers, including a white coffee planter and his black mistress, a young couple on their first trip to Africa who refuse to accept treatment from the local doctor, and Luc, an ex-priest who has gone native. Luc detects an attraction between France's mother Aimée and Protée, and taunts the latter. When Aimée makes a half-hearted attempt to seduce Protée, he turns her down and is banished, at Aimée's request, from the house to the garage, where France visits him secretly. The plane is finally repaired and the guests depart. France's reverie ends and she arrives at the airport. Mungo Park, assuming she is an ordinary tourist, asks if she is disappointed that he is not a real 'native'. (MFB, April 1989)

TIME OF THE GYPSIES

Yugoslavia 1989   Director: Emir Kusturica

Distributor: Enterprise; Production Company: Forum Film/Sarajevo TV; Executive Producer: Milan Martinovic; Producer: Mirza Pasic; Co-producer: Harry Saltzman; Screenplay: Emir Kusturica, Gordan Mihic; Photography: Vilko Filac; Editor: Andrija Zafranovic; Production Designer: Miljen Klajkovic; Music: Goran Bregovic.

Cast
Perhan: Davor Dujmovic; Ahmed Dzida: Bora Todorovic; Baba: Ljubica Adzovic; Uncle Merdzan: Husnija Hasmovic; Azra: Sinolicka Trpkova; Zabit: Zabit Memedov; Daca: Elvira Sali; Dzamila: Suada Karisik; Perhan's Son: Ajnur Redzepi.

Synopsis
Perhan, a teenage Gypsy with telekinetic powers, lives in a Yugoslav village with his grandmother Baba, his crippled younger sister Daca, and an indolent uncle, Merdzan. Perhan is in love with Azra, but her mother forbids the marriage. When Baba refuses to pay a gambling debt incurred in a card game with the visiting Ahmed Dzida, the village's richest Gypsy, Merdzan destroys their home in a fury, lifting off the roof and walls with a crane. Ahmed offers to pay for an

118

operation to straighten Daca's leg after Baba's magic heals his own child. Perhan accompanies Daca to Ljubljana, promising to stay with her in hospital, but Ahmed forces him to join his conscripted army of thieves and beggars on the outskirts of Milan. Perhan rises to become Ahmed's chief aide, and assumes control once Ahmed suffers a stroke. Against Ahmed's advice, he makes a return to Yugoslavia, where he finds no trace of Daca at the hospital, and no sign of the mansion which Ahmed was supposed to be building for him in the village. Azra, he discovers, is pregnant; Perhan agrees to marry her, but only if the child is sold at birth. Azra dies during labour; Perhan disowns the baby boy and returns, bitterly disillusioned, to Italy. Four years pass. Perhan hunts for his missing sister, and finds her in Rome, still crippled, begging for Ahmed, who is shortly to get married. He also discovers his own son among the urchins. After safely putting Daca and his son on a train to Yugoslavia, Perhan slips into Ahmed's wedding festivities and uses his telekinetic powers to kill him – only to be shot himself by Ahmed's enraged bride. At the funeral, gold coins are placed on Perhan's eyes; his son, true to his upbringing, creeps up and steals them. (MFB, April 1990)

YOUNG SOUL REBELS

United Kingdom 1991   Director: Isaac Julien

Distributor: BFI; Production Company: BFI for Film Four International, in association with Sankofa Film & Video, La Sept, Kinowelt, Iberoamericana; Executive Producers: Colin MacCabe, Ben Gibson; Producer: Nadine Marsh-Edwards; Screenplay: Paul Hallam, Derrick Saldaan McClintock, Isaac Julien; Director of Photography: Nina Kellgren; Editor: John Wilson; Production Designer: Derek Brown; Music: Simon Boswell.

Cast
Chris: Valentine Noyela; Caz: Mo Sesay; Ken: Dorian Healey; Ann: Frances Barber; Tracy: Sophie Okonedo; Billibud: Jason Durr; Davis: Gary McDonald; Jill: Debra Gillet; Carlton: Eamon Walker; TJ: Shyro Chung.

Synopsis
1977, during the week of the Queen's Silver Jubilee. Chris and Caz, close friends since childhood, are disc jockeys on a black pirate radio station called Soul Patrol, which broadcasts its 'funk' message from an East End garage. They are shocked by the death of their friend TJ, who

has been murdered while cruising the park by night, and Chris realises that a ghetto-blaster found in the park by his little sister contains a recording of the killer's voice.

Police investigating the murder visit the garage and question its owners, Davis and Carlton. Chris meanwhile talks his way into a commercial station, Mertro Radio, where he is refused a job but meets Tracy, a production assistant. He invites her that night to The Crypt, a club where the Soul Patrol are featured. The club turns out to be packed with blacks and whites, gays and straights, and soul boys who are soon at loggerheads with the local punks. Caz is disapproving of Tracy, whom he sees as interfering with Chris's commitment to Soul Patrol. Caz himself is attracted to a punk, Billibud, and when the Soul Patrol duo split up at the end of the evening, Chris leaves with Tracy and Caz later meets Billibud in the park.

While they are installing a new aerial for the station, supplied by a white friend Ken, Chris and Caz quarrel bitterly. Caz starts working with Billibud and their relationship develops into a sexual one, as does Chris's with Tracy. The police then arrest Chris for TJ's murder. He is released with Tracy's help, but the Soul Patrol station is broken into and vandalised: the murderer, clearly, is aware of the evidence on the tape. Afraid now for his life, Chris feels the absence of Caz. At a 'Stuff the Jubilee' concert in the park, Caz and Billibud are setting up their equipment when the arrival of National Front supporters results in a riot. Amidst the fire and violence, Caz and Chris finally confront and fight with TJ's murderer, Ken. The two friends are reunited and Soul Patrol resumes the air. (*Sight and Sound*, September 1991)